BRITISH RAIL
IN THE 1980s
AND 1990s
DIESEL LOCOMOTIVES
AND DMUs

Kenny Barclay

AMBERLEY

This book is dedicated to my loving grandmother, Elizabeth McBay,
who sadly passed away aged ninety-four years on Thursday 8 June 2017
while this book was in production.

First published 2017

Amberley Publishing
The Hill, Stroud
Gloucestershire, GL5 4EP

www.amberley-books.com

Copyright © Kenny Barclay, 2017

The right of Kenny Barclay to be identified as
the Author of this work has been asserted in
accordance with the Copyrights, Designs and
Patents Act 1988.

ISBN 978 1 4456 7005 8 (print)
ISBN 978 1 4456 7006 5 (ebook)

All rights reserved. No part of this book may be
reprinted or reproduced or utilised in any form
or by any electronic, mechanical or other means,
now known or hereafter invented, including
photocopying and recording, or in any information
storage or retrieval system, without the permission
in writing from the Publishers.

British Library Cataloguing in Publication Data.
A catalogue record for this book is available from
the British Library.

Origination by Amberley Publishing.
Printed in the UK.

Introduction

On 1 January 1948 the four main railway companies operating within Britain were nationalised. On this date British Railways was formed to take over the assets of the (GWR) Great Western Railway, (LNER) London & North Eastern Railway, (LMS) London, Midland & Scottish Railway and (SR) Southern Railway. The new nationalised British Railways was formed into six operating regions, these being Eastern Region, Western Region, Southern Region, Scottish Region, North Eastern Region and London Midland Region.

In December 1954 the 1955 Modernisation Plan was published, which proposed among other things the replacement of steam traction with diesel traction and investment in signalling and track, including the electrification of many main lines and the construction of large marshalling yards. The aim of the Modernisation Plan was to invest large amounts of money – quoted as being £1,240 million – into Britain's railways in order to bring them up to modern standards. It was hoped that this would in turn improve financial performance and get the railways back to profit by 1962.

In time the Modernisation Plan was regarded as a failure. The large marshalling yards were not required as the type of traffic that required marshalling – small wagonload traffic – was in serious decline. Many of the new classes of diesel traction introduced were unsuitable for the work for which they were purchased and other classes were horrendously unreliable. The last steam locomotives were built in 1960 and all would be withdrawn by 1968. By the end of the 1960s, a National Traction Plan had been drawn up, with many of the unreliable and non-standard classes of diesel locomotives being withdrawn shortly after. Between 1948 and 1964 car ownership within Britain increased dramatically, and road vehicle mileage grew at the rate of 10 per cent per year, which did little to revive British Railways' fortunes.

By 1961 British Railways was still losing money, which was recorded as being approximately £300,000 per day. The British Railways Board was formed in January 1963 to take over the running of the railways from the British Transport Commission. 1963 also brought the infamous Dr Beeching report, entitled *The Reshaping of British Railways*. In his report Dr Beeching proposed a reduction of 5,000 miles, which equated to 30 per cent of route miles, along with the closure of 2,363 stations, which was approximately 55 per cent of all stations. Most of the proposed closures were implemented, with the cuts taking place throughout the mid-1960s to early 1970s.

In 1965 British Railways was renamed British Rail and the famous double arrow logo was introduced, and a blue-based livery started to appear. The colour chosen was a dark grey-blue colour: Monastral blue, also known as Rail Blue. Locomotives and multiple units were painted in all-over blue with coaches also receiving a pearl grey vertical band lined out in white along the side panels. Locomotives and multiple units continued to receive yellow front ends to enable track workers to sight approaching trains. During the 1980s, multiple units also began to receive this blue and grey style of livery.

The 1970s saw the introduction of the successful HST (High Speed Train) fleet. It is safe to say this was a game changer for BR and revived the company's fortunes. Sadly, the other concept being developed by BR at the time, the APT (Advanced Passenger Train), was not a success story, and the few prototype APT units in service were withdrawn by 1985.

With the HST's arrival in 1976 it was decided to introduce a new style of livery that would better suit the aerodynamic lines of the new Class 43 power cars. This consisted of a greater area of yellow, extending along both sides of the locomotive. This livery suited the Class 43 locomotives well and in 1978 BR decided to introduce a new livery for the rest of the locomotive fleet. Known as BR Blue large logo livery, the livery consisted of a larger amount of yellow extending from the front of the locomotive to the sides as far as the cab doors. The cab windows were lined out in black and the locomotives were fitted with large, full-height BR double arrow logos. They also received larger fleetnumbers on both sides. The livery was well received and a welcome change to the drab BR all-over blue livery previously worn.

The 1980s were to be known as the sectorisation years and were to be colourful years. Since 1948, British Railways, latterly BR, had been organised into six regions. Beginning in 1982 this was changed and the regions were replaced by a number of business sectors, including: InterCity; London and Southeastern (later renamed Network SouthEast); Provincial (later renamed Regional Railways); Parcels (later renamed Rail Express Systems); Freightliner; Trainload Freight and Railfreight Distribution.

Long-distance passenger services would be operated by the InterCity sector. This would not be the first time the InterCity name was used. It was first used briefly in 1950 and again from 1966 onwards on services between the West Midlands and London. InterCity trains could be found operating from Aberdeen in the north-east of the country to Penzance in the south-west. InterCity operated Class 37, Class 43 and Class 47 diesel locomotives and also owned a number of Class 08 and Class 09 shunting locomotives. A new InterCity livery was introduced in May 1987. Based on the 'Executive' livery of dark and light grey with a red stripe and yellow cab fronts and sides introduced a few years earlier, the new InterCity livery consisted of white and dark grey with a red stripe and a silver Swallow logo. A new fleetname was also introduced, with InterCity being displayed as one word, no hyphen, and in italic serif font. By 1996 the InterCity sector had been privatised, with the network of services being divided up into several franchises. It was originally proposed to retain the InterCity brand, since by this time it had become very well-known and respected.

Passenger services in the London and South East area passed in 1982 to the London and South Eastern sector. This sector operated mostly commuter trains around the London area along with an inter-urban service in the densely populated South East of England, with a few services also extending west to Exeter. In June 1986 the sector was relaunched as Network SouthEast and introduced a new striking red, white and blue livery. The new branding was applied to both trains and stations, quickly becoming a household name, and was still carried on some trains as late as 2007. As well as operating a large fleet of EMUs, the sector also operated Class 33, Class 47 and Class 50 locomotives, along with both first and second generation DMUs, including Class 115, 117, 119, 121, 159, 165 and 166 units. When privatisation arrived in 1994, Network SouthEast was broken up into approximately eleven franchises, and had ceased to exist by 1997.

All other passenger services across Britain were operated by the Provincial sector. In Scotland the ScotRail name was carried. The Provincial sector was renamed Regional Railways in 1989. While both InterCity and Network SouthEast sectors were very profitable, the Provincial sector was not. When sectorisation was first introduced it required a subsidy four times greater than the revenue it generated. At first services were operated by first generation DMU trains and locomotive-hauled coaching stock, with some dating back to the 1950s and 1960s. Many of the vehicles were thought to contain asbestos, so it was decided that rather than remove the asbestos and refurbish the rolling stock, new second generation DMU units would be ordered. These fell into two categories: lightweight Pacer units built using Leyland National bus parts, and Sprinter units designed to operate long-distance services. Both the Pacer and Sprinter units were built by a variety of companies and featured different levels of comfort based on the services they were designed to operate. The Pacer units were designed to operate for no more than twenty years, but almost all built are still in service in 2017. Unless the Pacers receive major accessibility modifications by end of 2019, they will all have to be withdrawn from service as they will no longer comply with new regulations due to be introduced in 2020.

The massive influx of new rolling stock increased passenger numbers and by the end of the 1980s the subsidy required to run Regional Railways had reduced to two-and-a-half times its revenue. The Provincial sector introduced a two-tone blue livery with a white stripe, which was modified several times to suit each class of unit. By 1992 vehicles started to receive Regional Railways livery. This livery was very similar to the previous livery carried by the Sprinter units but had the addition of three short horizontal dark blue lines at the cab ends. Regional Railways operated a variety of diesel traction, including Class 31, Class 37 and Class 47 locomotives, Class 101, 117, 121 and Class 122 first generation DMUs, and Class 141, 142, 143, 144, 150, 153, 155, 156 and Class 158 second generation DMUs. The Class 153 units were produced using vehicles from Class 155 units. The final unit to carry Regional Railways livery was an East Midlands Trains Class 153, which carried the livery until July 2008. Upon privatisation in 1994 the sector was divided up into eight different franchises, which stretched the length of the country. The sector ceased to exist in March 1997.

As well as passenger services, new sectors were formed to look after parcels and freight. The Parcels sector was responsible for all parcels and mail traffic and was also responsible for the Travelling Post Office trains. The sector initially introduced a red and black Parcels sector livery with many vehicles retaining Post Office livery. The sector was renamed RES (Rail Express Systems) in 1991 and a new-style livery was introduced, which featured a predominantly red livery with a grey band extending three-quarters of the way along each side. The livery was finished with light blue and grey-painted boxes known as flashes on each side, intended to symbolise eagle wings. The livery was unveiled at an open day event held in October 1991 at Crewe Depot. A variety of traction repainted into the new livery was on show, which included Class 08, Class 47, Class 86 and Class 90 locomotives. Over time a large number of the Class 47/7 locomotives operated by RES received names beginning with the letters 'RES'. These included *Restless*, *Respected*, *Resolve* and *Respite*. As well as operating Class 08 and Class 47 locomotives, RES also operated first generation DMUs and parcel vans. By the early 1990s the DMUs had all been withdrawn and the remaining parcel vans had been refurbished. A fleet of new Class 325 EMU trains was introduced in 1995, which resulted in many of the RES Class 47 locomotives being stored. The company passed to EWS (English, Welsh and Scottish) Railways in 1996 and over time vehicles lost their RES livery.

The BR freight traffic passed initially into two sectors: Trainload Freight and Railfreight Distribution. Trainload Freight was responsible for bulk loaded train services and this accounted for approximately 80 per cent of BR's revenue from freight. It was sub-divided into four subsectors: Coal, Petroleum, Metals, and Construction. All four subsectors used the same two-tone grey livery, but each subsector fitted its own graphical markings to denote which subsector the locomotive belonged to. In 1989, 100 new Class 60 locomotives started to be delivered, which resulted in the withdrawal of many older locomotives. The company operated many classes of diesel locomotives, including Class 20, Class 26, Class 31, Class 33, Class 37, Class 47, Class 56, Class 58 and Class 60 locomotives.

In preparation for privatisation the sector was restructured in 1994 into three region-based companies: Loadhaul, Mainline Freight, and Transrail. At first the three new companies simply added their new company logos to the locomotives' current livery. However, over time Mainline Freight introduced a blue livery, with Loadhaul introducing a black and orange livery. Transrail decided to retain the old two-tone grey trainload freight livery, while simply replacing the subsector markings with Transrail red, white and blue logos. All three companies passed in 1996 to EWS (English, Welsh & Scottish) Railways, at which point locomotives began to receive EWS maroon and yellow livery.

The Railfreight Distribution sector was responsible for the rest of the BR freight services and included non-trainload, intermodal and freightliner services. In 1987 the company introduced a livery similar to the two-tone grey trainload freight livery. A red and yellow diamond logo was applied in a similar style to the subsector markings carried by trainload freight locomotives. In 1995 the intermodal part of the business was separated off to a new company called Freightliner, which was purchased by its management in 1996. It would go on to become the second largest freight operator in the UK. It is now a subsidiary of Genesee & Wyoming and currently operates in many countries around the world, as well as the UK. Railfreight Distribution introduced a revised version of their livery in 1992 to coincide with the planned opening of the Channel Tunnel in 1994. The revised livery featured a darker grey on the upper bodyside with a dark blue roof while larger Railfreight Distribution lettering was also carried on each side of the locomotives. Railfreight Distribution passed to EWS (English, Welsh & Scottish) Railways in 1997.

The 1980s and 1990s were interesting and colourful times for the railways in Britain. After years of being formed into regions with rolling stock painted either blue or blue and grey, BR restructured itself into business sectors. Over the next few years each sector introduced new trading names, logos and liveries. The changes were fast-paced and ultimately prepared British Rail for the privatisation process that began in 1994.

All the photographs within this book are my own work, captured over many years with my trusty Canon AE1 camera. At the time the photographs were taken I was employed by British Rail. I enjoyed the privilege of free staff travel and was therefore able to travel around the network, recording the changes in the fleet. I was also fortunate enough to gain regular access to a number of depots and works around the country, where again I could photograph the changes. I hope you enjoy this small selection that I have chosen from my collection just as much as I have enjoyed compiling this volume.

Kenny Barclay
June 2017

Class 03 Locomotive No. 03073

The Class 03 shunting locomotive was built by BR at both Doncaster and Swindon Works between 1957 and 1960. Fitted with a 204 hp Gardner 8L3 engine, a total of 230 were built, and withdrawals commenced in 1968. No. 03073 was originally No. D2073 and was constructed in 1959. In later life she was one of a number of locomotives to be fitted with dual brakes and by 1988 she had been allocated to Birkenhead Depot. She is pictured here at Crewe Depot on 12 October 1991, attending an open day event. Happily, No. 03073 lives on and is now a resident at Crewe Heritage Centre, where she is preserved in BR Blue livery.

Class 06 Locomotive No. 06003

The Class 06 shunting locomotive was built between 1958 and 1960 by Andrew Barclay, Kilmarnock. The locomotives were based in Scotland and No. 06003 was allocated to Kittybrewster, Aberdeen. Although they were all constructed by the same company, the first fifteen of the thirty-five locomotives were fitted with three cab windscreens, as seen with No. 06003. The remaining twenty were fitted with only two larger windows. By January 1973 only ten locomotives survived and these were renumbered from 06001–06010. The Class 06 locomotive was fitted with the same 204 hp Gardner 8L3 engine as the Class 03 shunting locomotive. Only one Class 06 locomotive remains, No. 06003, which is preserved in BR Blue livery. After withdrawal from normal service, No. 06003 passed to the Departmental fleet and saw work in the Reading area. After final withdrawal she was saved from Booths scrapyard in Rotherham and entered preservation. She passed through several owners and No. 06003 is now located at Rowsley as part of the Heritage Shunters Trust's collection. No. 06003 is pictured at Crewe Depot on 3 May 1997 during an open day event.

Class 08 Locomotive No. 08570

The most common British Rail shunting locomotive was the 350 hp Class 08 locomotive built between 1952 and 1962. In total 996 were constructed at many BR works, including at Crewe, Darlington, Derby, Doncaster and Horwich. The Class 08 locomotive could be seen up and down the country and in this photo No. 08570 is pictured in Edinburgh Waverley station wearing full InterCity livery, including Swallow logos. No. 08570 was new as No. D3737 on 8 May 1959 and was constructed at Crewe works. She was withdrawn in January 1992 and was scrapped at Motherwell depot during September 1993. By 2011, only around 100 Class 08 locomotives were still recorded being in active service.

Class 08 Locomotive No. 08578

No. 08578 was originally numbered D3745 and was new to traffic on 26 June 1959, being constructed by BR at Crewe works. Although shown as being withdrawn between 1981 and 1984, she went on to have a long working life and is recorded as working as late as 2011 with EWS Railways. The locomotive is currently shown as stored wearing EWS maroon and yellow livery. No. 08578 is pictured here at Newcastle station wearing Parcels red and dark grey livery. She was named *Lybert Dickinson* in November 1990.

Class 08 Locomotive No. 08633

British Rail was restructured into sectors during the 1980s. In 1991 the Parcels sector was renamed Rail Express Systems (RES) and introduced a revised red and grey livery with black and blue markings. An open day event was held at Crewe depot on 12 October 1991, wherein No. 08633 was named *The Sorter* and was displayed wearing the new RES livery. No. 08633 was constructed by BR Derby works on 12 December 1959 and was originally numbered D3800. She is pictured approaching Crewe station, looking smart in her newly applied RES livery, and also carrying the Crewe diesel depot Cheshire Cat cast depot logo. No. 08633 went on to receive EWS maroon and yellow livery and is recorded as stored.

Class 08 Locomotive No. 08720

No. 08720 spent much of its time in Scotland and is recorded as being based at Inverness, Perth, Stirling, Haymarket, Craigentinny and Eastfield depots. Originally numbered D3888, she was constructed at BR Crewe works on 10 June 1960. Pictured here attending BRML Springburn works, No. 08720 is wearing blue Provincial livery with Haymarket depot logos. The Class 08 locomotives had a top speed of 15 mph but it was possible to haul them faster as long as the connecting rods were removed, as seen here with No. 08720. She later received Departmental grey livery and later in life also received EWS maroon and yellow livery. She is recorded as being withdrawn in February 2007 and was scrapped at Stockton in November 2007.

Class 08 Locomotive No. 08881

BRML Springburn works is the location of this photograph of No. 08881. She is pictured wearing Departmental grey livery with black cab doors, as applied in 1991. No. 08881 was new to Fort William depot in August 1961 as No. D4095. She was constructed at BR Horwich works and survived in service until 2012, spending most of her working life in Scotland. Upon withdrawal she entered preservation and currently operates on the Somerset & Dorset Railway at Midsomer Norton as No. D4095 and wearing green livery.

Class 09 Locomotive No. 09013

The Class 09 shunting locomotive was very similar to the Class 08 but was re-geared to give a top speed of 27 mph. Having a higher top speed meant that the class occasionally operated out on the main line rather than being confined to shunting. Between 1959 and 1962, twenty-six were constructed and most were allocated to the Southern Region. No. 09013 entered service in October 1961 after construction at BR Horwich works. Originally numbered D4149, No. 09013 had moved from Cardiff to Tinsley depot near Sheffield by 1990. She is pictured on 29 September 1990 at Tinsley depot during an open day event. Around this time Tinsley depot started applying unofficial painted names on their locomotives and No. 09013 can be seen carrying *Shepcote*. She has also retained her Southern Region high-level EMU-style brake pipes. In 1992, twelve Class 08 locomotives were converted to become further Class 09 locomotives. By 1997, No. 09013 had received grey Departmental livery. She is recorded as being withdrawn around September 2010. The author was passed for both Class 08 and Class 09 locomotives when employed at Ayr depot with EWS Railways. After our allocated Class 08 locomotive was withdrawn we received a Class 09 and the higher speed was greatly appreciated when shunting wagons from Falkland yard to Ayr depot via the main line. Pleasingly, ten of the original twenty-six Class 09 locomotives have been preserved.

Class 20 Locomotive No. 20043

British Rail ordered 228 Class 20 Locomotives, known as English Electric Type 1s. They were constructed between 1957 and 1968 at Vulcan Foundry, Newton-le-Willows, or at Robert Stephenson & Hawthorn, Darlington. The first 128 locomotives were fitted with disc-style indicators, as can be seen on No. 20043, while the later locomotives received headcode boxes. No. 20043 was constructed at Vulcan Foundry in November 1959. She was initially allocated to Norwich depot and carried fleetnumber D8043. She is pictured at Tinsley depot wearing BR Blue livery during an open day event, which took place on 29 September 1990. Recorded as being withdrawn during June 1991 at Thornaby depot, she was scrapped by MC Metals, Glasgow, in March 1995.

Class 20 Locomotive No. 20137

The Class 20 locomotives could often be found working 'nose to nose' in pairs as seen in this photo. She is pictured wearing original Railfreight grey red stripe livery that a number of this Class received, alongside sister No. 20099, which still carries BR Blue livery. Being a later locomotive, No. 20137 is fitted with a headcode box. New in April 1966 as No. D8137, she was constructed at English Electric's Vulcan Foundry works. She was first allocated to Bescot depot and then, after a short period at Toton depot, spent most of the next eighteen years in Scotland, where she was allocated to both Eastfield and Haymarket depots. After being withdrawn in December 1992, she entered preservation on the Gloucestershire & Warwickshire Railway in 1994, and wears BR green livery.

Class 20 Locomotive No. 20190

No. 20190 began life as No. D8190 after construction at English Electric's Vulcan Foundry on 28 January 1967. She is pictured wearing BR Blue livery and is unusually marshalled 'nose first'. She passed to DRS in July 1997 and in April 1998 was renumbered to 20310. Withdrawal is recorded as 28 February 2013 and she was scrapped by Booths of Rotherham in June 2013.

Class 20 Locomotive No. 20196

Visitors to Toton depot between 1990 and 1992 would be greeted with a long line of withdrawn Class 20 locomotives. Pictured on 12 June 1992, No. 20196 is pictured in BR Blue livery at the head of one of the lines, awaiting her fate.

Class 20 Locomotive No. 20215

No. 20215 is pictured at Doncaster station on 1 September 1991 and is painted in original Railfreight grey red stripe livery. She is the leading locomotive working a special service from Worksop depot during an open day event, with sister locomotive No. 20142 painted in BR Blue livery behind. New in May 1967 as No. D8315, she was withdrawn in October 2009 and was scrapped shortly after at Booths of Rotherham.

Class 20 Locomotive No. 20217

MC Metals, Glasgow, is the location of this photograph of a sorry looking No. 20217. MC Metals occupied a yard next to BRML Springburn and was involved in the scrapping of many items of BR rolling stock. The company also specialised in asbestos removal at the time. The initials 'MC' stand for McWilliam & Christie, which were associated with former railway scrapyards in the Glasgow area. No. 20217 was new in November 1967 and was an early withdrawal in July 1989. She is recorded as being scrapped in February 1991. The SPT-liveried Class 156 in the background, No. 156 504, is not awaiting scrapping, but rather repair at BRML Springburn after a shunting accident.

Class 20 Locomotive No. 20904

Hunslet Barclay of Kilmarnock purchased and operated a fleet of six former BR Class 20 locomotives. They were normally used on summer weedkilling trains, 'top and tailed'. They received a smart two-tone grey livery with black lettering. No. 20904 started life as No. D8101 in November 1961 before becoming No. 20101 in December 1973. She was withdrawn in 1988 but was then sold and reinstated in 1989 as No. 20904, receiving the name *Janis* until 1998. No. 20904 later passed to DRS, receiving DRS blue livery, before passing to Harry Needle Railroad Co. By 2009 she was in storage at Barrow Hill in unbranded DRS blue livery. No. 20904 *Janis* is pictured during her time with Hunslet-Barclay at the head of a weedkilling train.

Class 24 Locomotive No. D5054

The Class 24 locomotives, also known as Sulzer Type 2s, were built between 1958 and 1961 at BR Darlington, Derby and Crewe works. Of the 151 built only four now survive, all in preservation. No. 24054 is pictured wearing BR green livery at an open day event while carrying her original number D5054. She was withdrawn from normal traffic in 1976 and was one of two Class 24 locomotives converted into train pre-heat units. Final withdrawal came in 1982. She is now based at the East Lancashire Railway, Bury, after arriving there in 1987. She carries the name *Phil Southern* after an early member and former director of the railway and is currently undergoing an overhaul.

Class 25 Locomotive No. D7541

No. D7541 is a Class 25 locomotive, also known as a Sulzer Type 2. There were 327 Class 25 locomotives constructed. No. D7541 was built at BR Derby works in 1965 and was originally allocated to Toton depot. She was withdrawn from service at Crewe depot in March 1987 and entered preservation on the North Yorkshire Moors Railway in January 1988. In 1992 she was repainted back into BR green livery from BR Blue livery and was also renumbered from 25191 back to D7541. In April 2011 she was sold to the South Devon Railway at Buckfastleigh and is currently undergoing overhaul. No. D7541 is pictured freshly painted in BR green livery at Thornaby depot on 20 September 1992 during an open day event.

Class 25 Locomotive No. 25235

No. 25235 is pictured in the scrapyard of MC Metals, Glasgow. Although looking in poor condition, it would appear someone must have taken notice of the 'help' marked on the side of the cab, since No. 25235 is still with us and part of the collection at the Scottish Railway Preservation Society, Bo'ness. The Class 25 locomotives were known as 'Rats', since they could be seen just about anywhere in the UK and were, therefore, as common as rats!

Class 25 Locomotive No. 97251

Originally numbered D7655 when constructed in July 1966 by Beyer Peacock, Manchester, this locomotive later became No. 25305. Withdrawn in April 1981, it was not the end of the road for this Class 25 as she was one of three Class 25 locomotives converted in 1983 to ETH generator vehicles. These were non self-propelled locomotives used to provide electric train heating when working with non-ETH locomotives. They were referred to as ETHEL (Electric Train Heating Ex-Locomotives) and received Departmental fleet numbers. No. 97251 (ETHEL 2) is pictured wearing Mainline livery outside Inverness depot. Note that grills have been fitted over both cab windscreens. Final withdrawal came in 1990 and she is recorded as being scrapped by MC Metals, Glasgow, in 1994.

Class 26 Locomotive No. 26002

A total of forty-seven Class 26 locomotives were built by Birmingham Railway Carriage & Wagon Co., Smethwick, between 1958 and 1959, with most ending up being based in Scotland. No. 26002 was new in October 1958 as No. D5302 and remained in service until October 1992. In November 1994 she entered preservation at the Strathspey Railway, Aviemore, and is currently awaiting overhaul. No. 26002 is pictured wearing Railfreight Coal livery inside BRML Springburn works, undergoing overhaul.

Class 26 Locomotive No. 26003

No. 26003 is pictured freshly painted in Railfreight Coal livery a long way from home. She is pictured at Worksop, taking part in an open day event on 1 September 1991. She later received 'Dutch Livery' – Departmental grey with a yellow band – and is recorded as being withdrawn in October 1993. Scrapping took place at MC Metals, Glasgow, in January 1995.

Class 26 Locomotive No. 26005.

The Class 26 locomotives were reliable workhorses. After refurbishment in the late 1980s, it was planned to keep the remaining thirty-three locomotives in service until as long as 2000. However, a few examples unfortunately suffered minor fire damage. No. 26005 is pictured at BRML Springburn works with a sister Class 26 locomotive, with both showing evidence of fire damage. Withdrawal took place in October 1993, with scrapping taking place at MC Metals, Glasgow, in February 1995.

Class 26 Locomotive No. 26028

No. 26028 was constructed in April 1959 and is pictured in BR Blue livery at the BR Civil Engineers yard, Shettleston, Glasgow. The author worked here in the late 1980s and although On-track Machines were a common sight within the yard, locomotives were very rare. No. 26028 never received a sectorisation livery and was withdrawn in October 1991. Scrapping is recorded as taking place at MC Metals, Glasgow, in November 1992.

Class 26 Locomotive No. 26032

New to traffic in February 1959 as No. D5332, No. 26032 is pictured wearing original Railfreight grey red stripe livery. In the background can be seen postal stock painted in both Royal Mail and Rail Express Systems livery. In this photo No. 26032 has lost her Railfreight logo from the cabside but still retains her Eastfield Terrier dog logo. Withdrawal came in October 1993 and she was scrapped by MC Metals, Glasgow, in February 1995.

Class 26 Locomotive No. 26039

A sorry-looking No. 26039 is pictured in the yard of MC Metals, Glasgow, still wearing BR Blue livery, accompanied by a Class 20 that is also in BR Blue livery. New in September 1959 as No. D5339, she was withdrawn earlier than other Class 26 locomotives in October 1990, and she was recorded as scrapped by October 1993. The last Class 26 locomotives in service were withdrawn in October 1993.

Class 26 Locomotive No. 26043

Thirteen of the forty-seven Class 26 locomotives built have entered preservation. One of the thirteen lucky ones, No. 26043, is pictured in Platform 6 at Perth station wearing Dutch livery. This was Departmental livery with the addition of a yellow stripe and dramatically improved the look of Departmental locomotives. No. 26043 now resides at Gloucestershire Warwickshire Railway in BR Blue livery. She was new to traffic as No. D5343 in October 1959 and was withdrawn in January 1993.

Class 26 Unidentified Locomotive

An unidentified Class 26 locomotive is pictured at MC Metals, Glasgow, awaiting her fate. She is pictured wearing original Railfreight grey red stripe livery, which many of the class wore. MC Metals was responsible for the scrapping of the majority of the Class 26 locomotives.

Class 27 Locomotive No. D5353

New to traffic as No. D5353 in September 1961, she was initially allocated to Eastfield depot in Glasgow. In March 1980, now renumbered 27007, she was allocated to Inverness depot. Withdrawal came in January 1985 after a minor battery fire, but that was not the end for No. 27007. She was purchased by the Mid Hants Railway in October 1985 but experienced another fire in 1986. She eventually entered service on the preserved line in 1992 and ran until 2000, when she was withdrawn for overhaul. Pictured in BR green livery, No. D5353 can be seen in the company of a Class 50 locomotive in Network SouthEast livery at an open day event.

Class 31 Unidentified Locomotive

An unidentified Class 31 locomotive is pictured wearing Departmental grey livery with black cab doors at Manchester Victoria station. Known as Brush Type 2 locomotives, 263 Class 31s were constructed by Brush Traction between 1957 and 1962. Originally fitted with either 1,250 hp or 1,365 hp engines, the entire fleet was fitted with English Electric 12SVT engines between 1965 and 1969 as fitted to Class 37 locomotives. Some members of the class remained in service with Network Rail until early 2017.

Class 31 Locomotive No. 31134

New to traffic as No. D5552 in September 1959, she was one of forty Class 31 locomotives to be built without roof-mounted headcode boxes, which received the nickname 'skinheads' as a result, although the first twenty skinheads were actually Class 31/0 locomotives. All Class 31/0 locomotives were withdrawn by the late 1970s, as they were regarded as non-standard. No. D5552 was renumbered 31134 with the introduction of TOPS and she survived until January 2000, when she was scrapped at Wigan Springs Branch depot. At the time Wigan Springs Branch depot was known as a component recovery depot, wherein components would be removed from withdrawn locomotives prior to scrapping.

Class 31 Unidentified Locomotive

An unidentified Class 31 in BR Blue livery is pictured awaiting her fate at MC Metals, Glasgow, in the company of a Class 45 locomotive and some InterCity-liveried Mk 2 coaches. She is already missing a panel from the front corner and some bodyside grills.

Class 31 Locomotive No. 31233

No. 31233 is pictured in Railfreight Petroleum livery and carries the name *Philips-Imperial*. Between 1993 and 1999 she was also named *Severn Valley Railway*. New in October 1960 as No. D5660, this locomotive remained in service with Network Rail until early 2017. She was one of four purchased by Network Rail from Fragonset and from 2015 was the sole remaining example still in use. Currently painted in Network Rail all-over yellow livery, in the past she has also worn Departmental Dutch grey and yellow.

Class 31 Locomotive No. 31400

This locomotive was built by Brush Traction of Loughborough in January 1960 as No. D5579. She was later renumbered 31161 and is pictured here carrying her final fleet number, 31400. She received this number in May 1988 after receiving ETH equipment. She was the first of seventy Class 31 locomotives to be fitted with ETH and be renumbered as Class 31/4 locomotives. She is recorded as being withdrawn in October 1991 and was scrapped by Booths of Rotherham in August 1993.

Class 31 Locomotive No. 31412

No. 31412 is pictured wearing Departmental grey livery at the head of a passenger train at Blackpool North station. New as No. D5692 in March 1961, No. 31412 was later renumbered 31512 in October 1990 when her ETH was isolated. At some point she has received front-end damage at the second man's side, which has resulted in a missing lamp bracket. A new lamp bracket has been fitted higher up, in the centre. Withdrawn in May 2006, she was scrapped shortly after by Ron Hull in Rotherham.

Class 31 Locomotive No. 31423

Freshly painted and looking smart in Mainline livery, No. 31423 is pictured hauling a passenger train at Preston station. The leading coach is a BR Mk 1 coach painted in Network SouthEast livery. The locomotive carried the name *Jerome K. Jerome* between 1990 and 1997, being named after the English writer born in Walsall, in the Midlands. The locomotive also carries depot code '3C' on the front, which denotes Ryecroft, Walsall. At the time of the photo she was actually allocated to nearby Bescot depot and was new to BR in June 1960 as No. D5621. Withdrawal came in February 2007 and she initially passed to Harry Needle Railroad Co. Later, in June 2009, she passed to TJ Thomson, Stockton-on-Tees, where she was scrapped in October 2009.

Class 31 Locomotive No. 31439

No. 31439 was the first class 31 to receive Regional Railways livery and is pictured fresh from the paint shop at Doncaster works open day on 12 July 1992. She was new in November 1960 as No. D5666 and later carried fleetnumber 31239 before being renumbered to 31439 in 1984. Over time she passed to EWS and was then acquired by Fragonset Railways in 1999. For many years she was stored at Meldon Quarry, Devon, and as late as 2007 was still wearing her Regional Railways livery. She then received a partial repaint into a plain blue livery and spent a few more years being stored at Long Marston before being scrapped by Booths of Rotherham in March 2011.

Class 31 Locomotive No. 31442 and No. 31413

No. 31442 and No. 31413 are pictured passing through Crewe station on a passenger train working. The first coach is a BR Mk 2 wearing Regional Railways livery. No. 31413 is wearing a non-standard livery of BR Blue with yellow cabsides and a light blue stripe along the bottom of the sides that changes to a red stripe around the cabsides. She carried the name *Severn Valley Railway* between 1988 and 1993. No. 31442 was new as No. D5679 in December 1960, later receiving fleetnumber 31251 before being numbered 31442. She was withdrawn in September 1993 and initially entered preservation before being scrapped by Booths of Rotherham in September 2004. No. 31413 was new as No. D5812 in August 1961 and is recorded as being withdrawn in May 1997, being scrapped at Doncaster in July 1997.

Class 31 Unidentified Locomotive

An unidentified Class 31 locomotive is pictured wearing original Railfreight grey with red stripe livery. This livery, which suited the lines of these locomotives very well, began to appear in 1982, initially on Class 20 and Class 58 locomotives. By 1987 the Railfreight sector had been subdivided into businesses and a new two-tone grey livery with an appropriate decal for the allocated business started to appear.

Class 31 Locomotive No. 31970

No. 31970 is pictured after withdrawal at Crewe. She is pictured wearing Railway Technical Centre red, white and blue livery. Constructed in October 1962 as No. D5861, she later became No. 31326 before receiving Departmental fleetnumber 97204 in May 1987. In September 1989 she was renumbered back into the normal fleet as No. 31970, but retained her Railway Technical Centre livery. Withdrawal came in September 1991 and she is recorded as being scrapped in March 1997.

Class 31 Unidentified Locomotive

An unidentified Class 31 locomotive is pictured at London Liverpool Street station wearing the later version of Departmental grey livery with added yellow. This livery became known as Dutch livery. The locomotive is pictured wearing the Stratford depot Sparrow cast logo.

Class 33 Locomotive No. 33030

The Class 33 locomotives were built by Birmingham Railway Carriage & Wagon Co. between 1960 and 1962. They were known as BRCW Type 3 locomotives and an initial batch of eighty-six locomotives, later known as Class 33/0s, arrived first. Later, a second batch of twelve, known as Class 33/2s, were delivered, making a total of ninety-eight locomotives being built. All entered service in the BR Southern Region. Being built by Birmingham Railway Carriage & Wagon Co. meant they were similar in appearance to both Class 26 and Class 27 locomotives. However, since they were built for the Southern Region, they were fitted with two-digit headcode blinds. No. 33030 was new to traffic in April 1961 as No. D6548. She is pictured here wearing BR Blue livery, now numbered 33030. In later life she carried Departmental Dutch livery, EWS maroon and yellow livery, and DRS livery. She was acquired by West Coast Railways from DRS Railways in September 2005 and still exists today, being stored at Carnforth in a withdrawn status as a source of spares.

Class 33 Locomotive No. 33042

No. 33042 is pictured a long way away from her normal territory. She is pictured at Sheffield station on 29 September 1990 with sister No. 33207 at the head of 'The Sulzer Rose' railtour, which headed to Sheffield for the Tinsley depot open day. She is pictured wearing Railfreight Construction livery, which many Class 33s carried around this time. She was new in July 1961 as No. D6560 and was withdrawn in October 1996. She is recorded as being scrapped on-site at Stewarts Lane depot, London, in January 1997.

Class 33 Locomotive No. 33058

New to traffic as No. D6577 in November 1961, she later received fleetnumber 33058. Towards the end of her working life, she was kept smart in BR Blue livery and could be found working many railtours up and down the country, as well as attending many open day events. She is pictured looking immaculate inside Stewarts Lane depot in 1991 but was withdrawn shortly after. She is recorded as scrapped at Booths of Rotherham in June 1994.

Class 33 Locomotive No. 33114

In 1968, nineteen Class 33 locomotives received a modified version of push-pull equipment at Eastleigh works. Their changed appearance earned them the nickname 'Bagpipes'. It was originally planned to number the converted locomotives as Class 34s, but instead they were numbered Class 33/1 locomotives. New in November 1960 as No. D6532, she carried two nameplates over the years. She was named *Sultan* between 1988 and 1989 before being renamed *Ashford 150* between 1992 and her withdrawal in 1993. She is recorded as being scrapped by MRJ Phillips at Eastleigh in August 1998. No. 33114 is pictured looking smart in revised Network SouthEast livery and carries a Spitfire depot plaque for her home depot, Eastleigh.

Class 33 Locomotive No. 33115

No. 33115 was new as No. D6533 in December 1960. She was withdrawn in May 1989 with a seized engine and shortly after became a Departmental locomotive numbered 83301 following conversion at Doncaster works. She received Mainline livery and became a 'dead load' fitted with Eurostar bogies, including third rail collection shoes for testing purposes. She was selected for this role since she was already wired for push-pull work. The testing consisted of providing power from the third rail via her Eurostar bogies to a Class 73 locomotive, No. 73205, at speeds up to 90 mph. A 4TC four-car multiple unit completed the test train. She is pictured at Ashford depot during an open day event on 6 June 1992 in the company of No. 73205. Recorded as withdrawn in 1994, she was disposed of to St Leonards Railway Engineering and was recorded as scrapped in 1996.

Class 33 Locomotive No. 33117

No. 33117 is pictured at the rear of Stewarts Lane depot, London, in BR Blue livery. She entered service in December 1960 as D6536 and remained in traffic until she was withdrawn in February 1997. She then entered preservation in March 1997 and is currently recorded as wearing BR Blue livery on the East Lancashire Railway. The Class 33/1 locomotives were all fitted with push-pull multiple working equipment, as seen on No. 33117. One of the duties the Class 33/1 locomotives were required to undertake was to operate trains on the Weymouth Harbour Tramway down to the Quay over a public road. A requirement was that the locomotive was fitted with a bell and a flashing light; this was fitted to the front of the Class 33/1 locomotive upon arrival at Weymouth and was plugged into the small socket that can be seen clearly in this photograph of No. 33117.

Class 33 Locomotive No. 33201

The second batch of Class 33 locomotives, Class 33/2s, were built 7 inches narrower to permit them to work through tunnels on the Tunbridge Wells and Hastings line. Being built to a narrower width earned them the nickname 'Slim Jims'. No. 33201 was new in February 1962 as No. D6586 and she is pictured wearing Departmental Dutch livery at Stewarts Lane Depot, London. Out of the ninety-eight Class 33 locomotives built, almost thirty have been preserved, including No. 33201, which now resides on the Swanage Railway in BR Blue livery.

Class 37 Locomotive No. 37051

One of the most successful locomotives ordered by BR were the Class 37s. They were ordered in seven batches between 1960 and 1965, with a total of 309 constructed. Known as English Electric Type 3s, they were constructed by English Electric at Vulcan Foundry, Newton-le-Willows, or Robert Stephenson & Hawthorn at Darlington. The first 119 locomotives, including No. 37051, had a split headcode box fitted to the front. This allowed a set of doors to be fitted on the nose which could allow train crew to pass from one locomotive to the other, assuming both had nose doors fitted! No. 37051 spent time operating within the Scottish Region; however, it is pictured here passing through Crewe station double-headed with another Class 37. She is wearing Railfreight Metals livery. New as No. D6751 in August 1962, she was part of the second batch ordered and was constructed at Vulcan Foundry. She carried the name *Merehead* from 1996 and is recorded as withdrawn in December 2007. She was scrapped by Sims Metals of Beeston in January 2008, by which time she was wearing EWS maroon and yellow livery.

Class 37 Locomotive No. 37106

No. 37106 was another split headcode box Class 37. She also has her warning horns built into the nose behind the two round grills. Later, Class 37s had the horns mounted on the roof. She is pictured wearing Railfreight Metals livery and is hard at work on the West Coast Main Line in Lanarkshire. She has also been fitted with the Eastfield depot plaque, which depicts the Highland Terrier. New as No. D6806 in January 1963, she later received Departmental Dutch livery. By May 2000 she had moved to Wigan Springs Branch depot for component recovery.

Class 37 Locomotive No. 37128

A sorry-looking No. 37128 is pictured at BRML Springburn works awaiting repair after having been involved in a collision with an engineer's train just outside Wemyss Bay station. She was new to traffic in June 1963 as No. D6828 and was one of many Class 37 locomotives to be constructed at Robert Stephenson & Hawthorn, Darlington, before the works closed in 1964. She carried Tinsley depot's unofficial name *Jupiter* between October 1992 and 1994 and was also renumbered as 37330 in 1994. She carried BR Blue large logo livery until withdrawal and spent many years stored at Toton depot. She is recorded as finally being scrapped in 2001.

Class 37 Locomotive No. 37139

Another photograph taken at BRML Springburn works. This time we see an immaculate No. 37139 fresh from the paint shop in Railfreight Coal livery. This would be the last repaint this particular locomotive would receive. This locomotive was constructed in May 1963 and was originally numbered D6839. Earlier in life she received a nasty head-on collision at Grangemouth causing considerable damage. Although officially shown as withdrawn in 2003, she was actually stored for many years before this at Thornaby depot. She was scrapped by TJ Thomson, Stockton-on-Tees, in February 2004.

Class 37 Locomotive No. 37153

No. 37153 is pictured awaiting entry into BRML Springburn works. She is wearing BR Blue large logo livery and also carries the Highland Railway Stag logo on her cabside, as was applied to many Scottish locomotives. She spent many years based in Scotland, including Inverness depot, and could often be found on the Inverness to Kyle of Lochalsh or Perth lines. She would emerge from the works wearing Departmental Dutch livery. Later she had Transrail logos added and this was the livery she would carry until withdrawal. Upon withdrawal she passed to Wigan Springs Branch depot for component recovery and the final disposal of her remains was to Booths of Rotherham in January 2003.

Class 37 Locomotive No. 37188

New to traffic in January 1964 as No. D6888, she was later renumbered 37188. In 1985 she was named *Jimmy Shand* at an event in Oban and she carried the name until 1989. In this picture of No. 37188 taken at Perth station she is seen wearing Railfreight Petroleum livery, and would later receive Departmental Dutch livery. No. 37188 was withdrawn in March 2006 and entered preservation. She is currently undergoing restoration work at Peak Rail, Derbyshire.

Class 37 Locomotive No. 37229

Fresh from the paint shop at BRML Springburn works Railfreight Coal liveried No. 37229 is pictured 'clearing her throat' while being started up. A Class 303 EMU in Strathclyde PTE livery can be seen in the background. She was constructed in February 1964 as D6929. Over the years she has carried three names: *Loch Arkaig*, *The Cardiff Rod Mill* and *Jonty Jarvis 8 12 1998–18 3 2005*. Jonty Jarvis was a young boy who tragically died at the age of six from meningitis. The locomotive passed to DRS and received DRS blue livery. Withdrawal came in August 2013 and she was scrapped shortly after at Booths, Rotherham.

Class 37 Locomotive No. 37262

Most locomotives that received the Departmental livery later received an additional yellow stripe, known as Dutch livery. No. 37262, however, remained in plain grey livery. She is pictured later in life at Eastleigh still carrying her *Dounreay* nameplates, which she received at Thurso in June 1985. New as No. D6962 in January 1965, she would end up with DRS, although she would never receive DRS livery. She is recorded as being withdrawn in October 2003 and was scrapped a few months later by Sims Metals, Beeston.

Class 37 Locomotive No. 37406

Thirty-one Class 37 locomotives were refurbished during 1985 and 1986 at Crewe works. During this work they were fitted with ETH equipment and their English Electric generators were replaced with Brush BA1005A alternators. After they emerged from the works they were renumbered into the Class 37/4 series, with the majority being allocated to Scotland. No. 37406 was new to traffic as No. D6995 in July 1965 and after the 1973 TOPS renumbering she became No. 37295. She carried many liveries over the years, including BR Blue large logo, Mainline, Railfreight Distribution, Transrail and finally EWS maroon and yellow. She was named *The Saltire Society* in 1986 and here she is pictured at BRML Springburn works wearing Mainline livery. Unusually she has been fitted with part of her fleetnumber, '406', on the front nose. Withdrawal took place in October 2012 and she is recorded as being scrapped by Booths of Rotherham in May 2013.

Class 37 Locomotive No. 37407

Sister Class 37/4 locomotive No. 37407 is pictured inside BRML Springburn works undergoing an overhaul and repaint into Mainline livery. She has still to receive yellow front ends and fleet numbers. She entered service as No. D6605 in October 1965. She then carried fleetnumber 37305 before becoming No. 37407 after refurbishment. She carried the name *Loch Long* between 1986 and 1995 and after transfer from Eastfield depot to Crewe Diesel depot she was renamed *Blackpool Tower*. Over the years she has also carried a number of liveries, including BR Blue large logo, Mainline, Transrail and EWS maroon and yellow. Happily she is still around today as part of the DRS fleet and in March 2017 she received BR Blue large logo livery.

Class 37 Locomotives No. 37413 and No. 37407

No. 37413 is pictured with sister No. 37407 completing a shunt movement at Platform 2 of Inverness station, a location the author knows very well. No. 37413 is pictured wearing Railfreight Distribution livery and carried the name *Loch Eil Outward Bound* until 1997, when she then received the name *The Scottish Railway Preservation Society,* which she kept until around the year 2000. She was delivered from English Electric in April 1965 as No. D6976 and in 1973 received fleetnumber 37276. After her 1985 refurbishment she became No. 37413. Over the years she carried BR Blue large logo, Railfreight Distribution, Transrail and finally EWS maroon and yellow. By 2008 she was withdrawn and stored at Margam but by 2010 she had entered preservation at Bo'ness with the Scottish Railway Preservation Society. After a number of years stored at Bo'ness she was moved back south and remained in storage at a number of locations, including RTC Derby, the East Lancashire Railway and Barrow Hill. Her future is uncertain, as her condition is poor after almost ten years in open storage.

Class 37 Locomotive No. 37416

Seen outside the paint shop at BRML Springburn works, No. 37416 is wearing Mainline livery. New in September 1965 as No. D6602, she later carried fleetnumber 37302 before receiving number 37416 in 1985 after her refurbishment. Between 1993 and 1999 she carried an unofficial name *Mt Fuji* and then in 2000 received the name *Sir Robert McAlpine* on one side and *Concrete Bob* on the other. This name was previously carried by No. 37425. In time she passed to EWS Railways and received standard maroon and yellow livery before receiving the Royal Scotsman livery of Royal Claret with Royal Scotsman branding. She was withdrawn in October 2012 and was scrapped by Booths of Rotherham in March 2013.

Class 37 Locomotive No. 37419

No. 37419 was new to traffic in June 1965 as No. D6991. After the TOPS renumbering in 1973 she received fleetnumber 37291 before receiving No. 37419 in 1985 after her refurbishment at Crewe works. She is pictured in Manchester Victoria station and carries Mainline livery. She later carried EWS maroon and yellow livery before becoming one of very few Class 37s to receive DB Schenker livery. Although DB had intended to use No. 37419 for further service, she suffered a serious engine fault shortly after being brought out of storage. She was then withdrawn by DB before passing to DRS, where she received DRS blue livery and remains as part of the DRS fleet today. She has carried the name *Carl Haviland 2012* since 2012 and previously carried an unofficial name *Mt Pinatubo* in 1993.

Class 37 Locomotive No. 37430

After conversion to Class 37/4s, the first twenty-five of the batch were allocated to Scottish depots. The final six, including No. 37430, were allocated to Cardiff Canton depot for use in Wales. However, No. 37430 is pictured a long way away from Wales at BRML Springburn works. She is wearing BR Blue large logo livery and would go on to also carry Mainline and Transrail liveries. In May 1986 she received the name *Cwmbran* after a town in Wales. If you look closely she also carries the VR depot code on her front windscreen. VR denotes the Vale of Rheidol Railway (Aberystwyth) steam depot. She also has her fleetnumber painted on the front which was unusual at this time. She entered service carrying fleetnumber D6965 in February 1965. In 1973 she was renumbered 37265 before receiving No. 37430 after her refurbishment in 1986. By 2002 she had been stored at Motherwell depot and was officially withdrawn in December 2007. Scrapping took place a few months later at EMR Kingsbury.

Class 37 Locomotive No. 37508

The Class 37/5 locomotives received a similar refurbishment to the Class 37/4 locomotives. Like the Class 37/4s, they received an alternator in place of the original generator. They did not, however, receive ETH equipment. When the refurbished locomotives were renumbered into the Class 37/5 series, the earlier split headcode box examples received numbers from 37501 upwards. The later single headcode box examples received fleetnumbers starting at 37699, numbered downwards. No. 37508 is pictured inside BRML Springburn works receiving an overhaul. She was new to traffic as No. D6790 in January 1963 and was constructed at Robert Stephenson & Hawthorn, Darlington, under contract to English Electric. During the TOPS renumbering in 1973 she received fleetnumber 37090 before becoming No. 37508 in 1986. This would not be the last number carried by this locomotive. In 1996 she was one of twelve Class 37 locomotives that were refurbished and fitted with ETH for EPS (European Passenger Services) with the intention of hauling overnight international trains. This plan was abandoned by 1997 and she would later pass to DRS, where she is still an active member of the fleet wearing DRS blue livery.

Class 37 Locomotive No. 37513

The Class 37 was classified as a Type 3 locomotive since they had a 1,750 hp English Electric 12CSVT engine fitted. No. 37513 is pictured in Railfreight metals livery and would later receive Loadhaul livery. She was previously numbered 37056 and would have therefore been fitted with nose doors that had been removed by the time this picture was taken. She entered service as No. D6756 in September 1962 and although officially recorded as withdrawn in October 2007, she spent many years prior to that stored at Old Oak Common depot, London. She was scrapped by Booths of Rotherham in February 2008.

Class 37 Locomotive No. 37694

Pictured at Eastfield depot in Glasgow, No. 37694 awaits her next duty in the company of a pair of Class 26 locomotives, Class 47 No. 47633 and a Class 08 locomotive. She was new as No. D6892 in February 1964 and was another Class 37 built by Robert Stephenson & Hawthorn, Darlington, under contract to English Electric. She later received fleetnumber 37192 before becoming No. 37694 in June 1986. Although carrying fleetnumber 37694, she was actually a Class 37/5. Between 1990 and 1993 she carried the name *The Lass O' Ballochmyle*, after the famous Robert Burns song, and was often found working Ayrshire coal trains. She is wearing Railfreight Coal livery, which she received prior to an open day event held at Doncaster works in May 1990, where she was a static exhibit fresh from the paint shop. She would later receive EWS maroon and yellow livery. She spent many years stored at Temple Mills and Old Oak Common depots. Officially withdrawn in October 2007, she was scrapped by EMR Kingsbury in January 2008.

Class 37 Locomotive No. 37719

The Class 37/7 subclass consisted of forty-four locomotives that were converted in the late 1980s. They all received the same refurbishment and their main generators were replaced with alternators, as with the Class 37/5 locomotives. The main difference with the Class 37/7 was the addition of approximately 12 tons of ballast weight. This was to improve the tractive effort or pulling power of the locomotives. They were again renumbered, with the early build locomotives that would have originally had split headcode boxes receiving lower numbers from 37701 to 37719, and the later build locomotives receiving fleetnumbers from 37899 downwards. No. 37719 entered service in March 1962 as No. D6733; she was renumbered 37033 in 1973 and in March 1989 was again renumbered as 37719. She is pictured in the bay platform at Warrington Bank Quay station wearing Railfreight Petroleum livery, which would be the final livery she would wear before withdrawal. She is officially shown as being withdrawn in December 2007 and was scrapped in January 2008 by EMR Kingsbury although she spent many years stored at Old Oak Common prior to this.

Class 37 Locomotive No. 37901

The last Class 37 subsector was the Class 37/9. In 1986, four Class 37 locomotives received Mirrlees MB275T engines and Brush alternators in place of their standard English Electric engines and generators, becoming Class 37/9 locomotives. This was to test the suitability of the new engine and alternator for a future build of new diesel locomotives. Later, in 1987, a further two Class 37 locomotives also became Class 37/9 after being fitted with Ruston engines and GEC alternators. During the conversion work the outside of these locomotives changed, with the loss of engine room windows and revised front grills and roof panels. They also received extra ballast weights to increase their weight to 120 tons, like the Class 37/7s. No. 37901 is pictured wearing Railfreight metals livery while stabled at Carlisle station. She carried the name *Mirrlees Pioneer* from December 1986 until 2002. Now preserved, she carries the name once again. She began life as No. D6850 in July 1963; ten years later she received fleetnumber 37150 before becoming No. 37901 in October 1986. Of the six Class 37/9 locomotives, three have been preserved, including No. 37901, which now carries original Railfreight grey livery with large BR logo.

Class 40 Locomotive No. D306

The English Electric Class 40 locomotives, also known as 'Whistlers', were built between 1958 and 1962. After an initial batch of ten, a further 190 were built. Similar in appearance to Class 37s, these locomotives were more powerful at 2,000 hp, making them Type 4 locomotives. All were built at English Electric's Vulcan Foundry, except a small batch of twenty-five, including No. D306, which were built at Robert Stephenson & Hawthorn, Darlington. No. D306 entered service in October 1960 and later received TOPS number 40106. She was withdrawn from service in April 1984 and is one of seven Class 40 locomotives now preserved. No. D306 is a resident on the East Lancashire Railway and is owned by the Class 40 Preservation Group. She received the name *Atlantic Conveyor* in 1984 and is pictured taking part in an open day event carrying a headboard for 'The Royal Scot'.

Class 42 Locomotive No. D821

Most diesel locomotives ordered by British Rail were diesel electric locomotives. The Western Region were keen to try diesel hydraulic locomotives and ordered a batch of thirty-eight Type 4 diesel hydraulic locomotives based on the German Federal Railway's V200 design. They were built between 1958 and 1961 at British Rail's Swindon works. All received names – most were named after Royal Navy ships and had 'Warship Class' in small letters under their main name. Due to their non-standard design and also due to limited space in the engine room preventing additional equipment to be installed for hauling modern coaches, the batch was withdrawn between 1967 and 1972. The early withdrawal resulted in none of the batch receiving or carrying TOPS fleetnumbers while in active service. No. D821 entered service in May 1960 and was withdrawn in November 1972. She is one of two locomotives now preserved and currently wears BR Maroon livery. Although originally named *Greyhound*, she has also carried the name *Chris Broadhurst*. No. D821 is pictured wearing BR Blue livery while taking part in an open day event.

Class 43 Locomotive No. 43036

Arguably the most successful diesel locomotive introduced by British Rail was the Class 43 HST power car. A total of 197 were constructed at BR Crewe works between 1975 and 1982. All but three remain in service, the three being scrapped after separate accidents on the Western Region. No. 43036 was new to traffic in January 1977 and is pictured at London Paddington station looking smart in InterCity livery. Behind, another Class 43 locomotive can be seen wearing the old style of InterCity livery.

Class 43 Locomotive No. 43065

In late 1987, when British Rail realised the new Mk 4 coaches for the East Coast Main Line would not be delivered in time, it was decided to convert eight Class 43 locomotives to work as Driving Van Trailers (DVT) with the new Class 89 and 91 locomotives. No. 43065 was one of those converted. The conversion work was carried out at Stratford works and involved removing the front lower valance and fitting buffers. The converted locomotives also received equipment to allow then to work in push-pull mode with the new East Coast electric locos. No. 43065 was new in October 1977 and has carried the name *City of Edinburgh* twice. After a period of storage, No. 43065 joined the Grand Central fleet in 2007 and, after receiving a new modern engine, received fleetnumber 43465. She is currently in service with Grand Central, based at Heaton depot near Newcastle. She is pictured after receiving her buffers in Leeds station, wearing InterCity livery and attached to a Mk 2 barrier vehicle, which is also wearing InterCity livery.

Class 43 Locomotive No. 43067

Another of the eight Class 43 locomotives to receive buffers, No. 43067 is pictured in York station at the head of a Mk 3 HST set. She has received a full yellow front end, which was carried initially by all eight of the converted Class 43 locomotives. New in November 1977 like her sister No. 43065, she also re-entered service in 2007 with Grand Central after many years of storage. She now carries fleetnumber 43467.

Class 43 Locomotive No. 43078

New to traffic in February 1978, No. 43078 is pictured in InterCity livery at Edinburgh Waverley station. She is currently based at Old Oak Common depot, London, and wears First Great Western Indigo Neon Blue livery. No. 43078 is part of the First Great Western fleet for services over the former BR Western region. Over the years she has carried Intercity, Virgin Trains, Midland Main Line, GNER and First Great Western liveries. She has also carried a number of nameplates, including *Rio Crusader*, *Golowan Festival Penzance* and *Shildon, County Durham* twice.

Class 43 Locomotive No. 43081

It is unusual to see a Class 43 locomotive operating on its own, due to having only one cab to drive from. No. 43081 is pictured in InterCity livery passing through Edinburgh Waverley station. It is more than likely this locomotive was being attached to a HST set to replace a defective HST power car. No. 43081 was new in March 1978 and is now in service with East Midland Trains. She briefly carried the name *Midland Valenta* in 2008 and has carried three different versions of the Midland Main Line/East Midland Trains livery over the years.

Class 43 Unknown Locomotive

Pictured wearing the original InterCity livery including 125 branding is an unidentified Class 43 at London Paddington station. The Class 43 was a 2,250 hp locomotive and holds the record for the fastest diesel locomotive in the world. Although normally restricted to 125 mph, they can reach 148 mph. When new they were all fitted with a Paxman Valenta 12RP200L engine. Between 1987 and 1996, four locomotives on the Western Region received trial Mirrlees MB190 engines. Many Class 43 locomotives went on to receive Paxman 12VP185L engines and, more recently, MTU V164000 engines.

Class 45 Unknown Locomotive

Between 1960 and 1962, 127 Class 45 locomotives were constructed. Known as BR Type 4s, they were constructed at both BR Derby and Crewe works. The majority of the fleet were withdrawn between 1981 and 1988 with the last withdrawn in 1989. Approximately fifty-five of the fleet were scrapped at MC Metals, Glasgow, where this unidentifiable locomotive is pictured awaiting her fate with some sister Class 45 locomotives.

Class 45 Unknown Locomotive

Another unidentifiable Class 45 pictured awaiting her fate at MC Metals, Glasgow. The Class 45 was based on an earlier batch of ten Class 44 locomotives produced in 1959. The Class 45s had a higher power rating of 2,500 hp, with the Class 44 locomotives having only 2,300 hp. A further fifty-six locomotives were built between 1961 and 1963 and became Class 46 locomotives. These locomotives received Brush equipment rather than the Crompton Parkinson equipment fitted to the Class 44 and Class 45 locomotives. All three classes were always known as 'Peaks', due to the fact that ten Class 44 locomotives received the names of English and Welsh mountains.

Class 45 Locomotive No. 45113

No. 45113 was constructed in December 1960 at Crewe works and originally carried fleetnumber D80. During her later years at Tinsley depot, near Sheffield, she received an unofficial painted name: *Athene*. She is recorded as being withdrawn in August 1988 and is pictured here in BR Blue livery, awaiting her fate at MC Metals, Glasgow.

Class 45 Locomotive No. 45135

There are eleven Class 45 locomotives in preservation, including No. 45135, which is seen here attending the Worksop open day event on 1 September 1991. She was new to traffic in May 1961 as No. D99, being constructed at BR Crewe works. She was withdrawn in March 1987 and is currently a resident on the East Lancashire Railway in BR Blue livery. She has carried the name *3rd Carabinier* since 1965.

Class 47 Unknown Locomotive

The Class 47 locomotive was built by Brush Traction and BR Crewe works between 1962 and 1968. Initially they had a power output of 2,750 hp and were known as Brush Type 4 locomotives; later, to improve reliability, their power was reduced to 2,580 hp. In total 512 were built, making it the largest class of main line locomotives built. Of the 512, 202 were built at Crewe, with the remaining 310 being built at Brush Falcon works, Loughborough. The Class 47 has proved to be a very successful and reliable locomotive. Despite being around fifty years old, in early 2017 thirty are still registered for main line work and a further thirty-two are currently preserved. An unidentifiable Class 47 is captured arriving at London Paddington station in InterCity livery, hauling a matching rake of Mk 2 InterCity coaches.

Class 47 Unknown Locomotive

Another unidentified Class 47, this time wearing Mainline livery, is pictured passing through Platform 1 at Crewe station, hauling an InterCity 125 HST. When first built the Class 47 locomotives were numbered from D1500 to D1999 and from D1100 to D1111. The first twenty locomotives built, numbered D1500 to D1519, were slightly different and were among the first to be withdrawn. All of the first twenty had been withdrawn by 1992.

Class 47 Locomotive No. 47110

Locomotives numbered between 47001 and 47298 were designated Class 47/0s and were fitted with steam heat equipment. No. 47110 was new to traffic in January 1964 as No. D1698. She was constructed by Brush at Falcon works, Loughborough. She is recorded as being withdrawn in May 1989 and was cut up on site at Thornaby in September 1993. She is pictured at Thornaby depot on 20 September 1992 during an open day event.

Class 47 Locomotive No. 47220

No. 47220 is pictured wearing original Railfreight grey livery while undergoing overhaul inside BRML Springburn works, Glasgow. This overhaul would be her last since she is recorded as being withdrawn in July 1993, a few years after this picture was taken. Between 1991 and 1993 she carried the unofficial Tinsley depot name of *Rapier*. Delivered to British Rail as No. D1870 in June 1965, she was constructed at Brush Falcon works, Loughborough, and she was scrapped by Coopers Metals, Attercliffe, Sheffield, in April 1994.

Class 47 Locomotive No. 47289

New to traffic in March 1966 as No. D1991, she later became No. 47289 during the 1973 TOPS renumbering. She is pictured in Railfreight Distribution livery passing through Carlisle station with a trainload of steel coils. She had a long career in service, later passing to Freightliner where she spent several years stored at Crewe before officially being withdrawn in July 2008. No. 47289 was scrapped in 2010 by TJ Thomson, Stockton-on-Tees.

Class 47 Locomotive No. 47301

The Class 47/3 subclass of locomotive were not fitted with either steam or electric train heat equipment; instead they were all fitted with slow speed equipment and were therefore mostly found on freight work. No. 47301 was new as No. D1782 in November 1964 and she is recorded as being withdrawn in January 2003 and scrapped at Crewe shortly after. Between 1991 and 1995, No. 47301 carried the unofficial Tinsley depot name of *Centurion* before receiving the name *Freightliner Birmingham* in November 1995. She is pictured awaiting her next duty at Edinburgh Waverley station and is wearing original Railfreight livery, complete with red stripe. She has been fitted with large fleetnumbers and the Kingfisher logo, which is associated with Thornaby depot.

Class 47 Locomotive No. 47306

No. 47306 was constructed in November 1964 by Brush at their Falcon works, Loughborough. She entered service as No. D1787. She is pictured in the yard at Toton depot and carries Railfreight Distribution livery. In 1994 she received the name *The Sapper* and in August 2000 she attended an open day event at Oak Common depot, freshly painted in Railfreight Distribution livery with large lettering. She later passed to EWS Railways and after many years in storage was sold to Harry Needle Railroad Co., Barrow Hill. In 2007 she moved to the Bodmin & Wenford Railway, Cornwall, where she entered service in 2008 still wearing her Railfreight Distribution livery.

Class 47 Locomotive No. 47328

No. 47328 is pictured at Inverness station, Platform 1, at the head of a SRPS railtour from Inverness to Edinburgh on 11 May 1991. She is wearing Railfreight Construction livery and at this time was allocated to Eastfield depot in Glasgow. She was new in January 1965 as No. D1809 and was scrapped at Booths of Rotherham in September 2005.

Class 47 Locomotive No. 47337

New into traffic as No. D1818 in February 1965, No. 47337 is pictured in platform 6 at Perth station wearing original Railfreight livery. On 24 April 1986 she received the name *Herbert Austin* at the Rover car plant at Longbridge to commemorate eighty years of car production at the site. She later received the unofficial Tinsley name *Taliesin*, which can be seen in this photograph. In November 2003 she returned to Brush at Loughborough to be rebuilt as a Class 57 locomotive. Thirty-three Class 47 locomotives received the rebuild between 1998 and 2004. During this rebuild she received a refurbished EMD engine and became No. 57602. The Class 57/6 locomotives were originally painted green with cast number and nameplates. No. 47337 was later repainted into First Great Western blue livery and in 2004 received the name *Restormel Castle*. She was normally to be found on Night Riviera sleeper service with the occasional empty stock move.

Class 47 Locomotive No. 47353

No. 47353 was constructed at Brush, Loughborough, in March 1965. She entered traffic as No. D1834 and carried this number until 1973 when she was renumbered 47353 under the TOPS renumbering scheme. She is pictured wearing Departmental grey livery complete with cast BR logos outside Doncaster works. She later went on to join the Freightliner fleet and when withdrawn in September 2004 she was wearing two-tone grey livery with Freightliner red triangle logo. She is recorded as being scrapped at Rotherham in February 2005 by Booths.

Class 47 Locomotive No. 47364

New to traffic as No. D1883 after construction at Brush, Loughborough, in July 1965, she later received TOPS number 47364. She is pictured at Old Oak Common depot, London, in the company of a sister Class 47 wearing Network SouthEast livery. She is wearing Departmental grey and yellow Dutch livery and appears to have received a new buffer recently.

Class 47 Locomotive No. 47364

A later view of No. 47364, this time at the head of a Railway Technical Centre test train at London Paddington station. In 1993 she was renumbered 47981, becoming part of the Railway Technical Centre fleet, and could often be found hauling test trains on the network. By 1999 she had been a victim of an engine room fire and was to be found at Wigan Springs Branch component recovery depot. She is recorded as being finally disposed of by May 2000.

Class 47 Locomotive No. 47475

The only Class 47 to receive Regional Railways' Provincial livery was No. 47475. New in July 1964 as No. D1603 after construction at Crewe works, she is pictured wearing her Provincial livery at Carlisle station. In 1993 she received the Parcels Sector Rail Express Systems livery and carried the name *Restive* until 2003. She was withdrawn in 2003 and spent many years in storage until finally being scrapped by TJ Thomson, Stockton-on-Tees, in March 2008.

Class 47 Locomotive No. 47476

Locomotives numbered in the Class 47/4 series were fitted with ETH (Electric Train Heat) and therefore were most suitable for hauling passenger trains. No. 47476 was new to traffic as No. D1604 in July 1964, being constructed at Crewe works. She is pictured wearing Parcels red and grey livery in the yard at BRML Springburn works, Glasgow. She later received the name *Night Mail* and is recorded as being withdrawn in February 2004, with scrapping taking place at Booths of Rotherham in May 2004.

Class 47 Locomotive No. 47484

Class 47/4 No. 47484 is pictured wearing GWR Brunswick Green livery inside Old Oak Common depot, London. The locomotive is undergoing some repair work to her front end. She was new in February 1965 as No. D1662 and was one of many Class 47 locomotives constructed at BR Crewe works. Almost since new she has carried the name *Isambard Kingdom Brunel*, being named after the famous civil and mechanical engineer born in April 1806. No. 47484 has been preserved by the Pioneer Diesel Locomotive Group and still wears her green livery. She has spent almost ten years in storage within a haulage yard at Wishaw, Sutton Coldfield, and the group report that they are awaiting a suitable location to commence her restoration.

Class 47 Locomotive No. 47512

New to traffic as No. D1958 in February 1967, No. 47512 is pictured outside BRML Springburn works, Glasgow. She is wearing BR Blue large logo livery, a livery she carried until she was withdrawn in October 1991. She then spent many years stored at Crewe depot before being scrapped by Booths of Rotherham in May 1994.

Class 47 Locomotive No. 47522

No. 47522 is pictured freshly repainted in Parcels red and grey livery at an open day event at Doncaster works on 12 July 1992. She was constructed at BR Crewe works in November 1966 and entered service as No. D1105. In May 1982 she was involved in a collision with a tractor near Perth. The impact was so serious the locomotive left the rails and summersaulted through the air, with the rear cab ending up embedded in the ground. Surprisingly she was repaired but in May 1990 was again in the wars and required another new cab to be fitted. In October 1987 she received LNER apple green livery with Parcels logos and was named *Doncaster Enterprise*. She is recorded as being withdrawn in December 1998 and spent a few years stored at Wigan Springs Branch component recovery depot prior to scrapping taking place.

Class 47 Locomotive No. 47525

Constructed in January 1967 at BR Crewe works, she entered service as No. D1108 shortly after. She is pictured wearing early InterCity livery at Chester station at the head of a passenger train complete with a Mk 1 guard van in matching InterCity livery. In 1995 she received Railfreight Distribution livery. By July 2008 she had spent a period of time stored with West Coast Railways at Carnforth and disposal would come in August 2010, when she was scrapped by EMR Kingsbury.

Class 47 Locomotive No. 47532

No. 47532 is pictured wearing Rail Express Systems livery at Carlisle station. She was new to traffic in December 1964 as No. D1641 and was one of many Class 47 locomotives constructed at Crewe works. She was renumbered to 47057 in 1973 and again in 1979 to become No. 47532. By 2000 she had been stored at Crewe depot, still wearing Rail Express Systems livery. She is recorded as being scrapped at Wigan Springs Branch component recovery depot in 2001.

Class 47 Locomotive No. 47578

New to traffic in October 1964 as No. D1776 after construction at Brush Loughborough, she was renumbered to 47181 in 1973 and she received the fleetnumber 47578 in 1981. In 1994 she was one of many Class 47/4 locomotives to be fitted with long-range fuel tanks and received fleetnumber 47776. She carried two different nameplates over the years. Between 1985 and 1991 she carried *The Royal Society of Edinburgh* and between 1991 and 2004 she was named *Respected*. For almost ten years this locomotive has been in storage at the West Coast Railways yard at Carnforth. In this photograph No. 47578 is pictured at BRML Springburn works, Glasgow, wearing BR Blue large logo livery, complete with *The Royal Society of Edinburgh* nameplates. An InterCity-liveried Motorail vehicle can be seen in the background.

Class 47 Locomotive No. 47598

No. 47598 is pictured approaching London Paddington station and wears the later version of Network SouthEast livery. She was new in November 1964 as No. D1777 following construction by Brush at Loughborough. In 1973 she received TOPS number 47182. In 1983 she was renumbered as 47598 and in 1995 she received fleetnumber 47742 after being fitted with long-range fuel tanks. She received Rail Express System livery in July 1992 and was named *The Enterprising Scot* in July 1995. She was scrapped by EMR Kingsbury in May 2007 after spending a few years stored at Toton depot.

Class 47 Locomotive No. 47630

No. 47630 is pictured wearing BR Blue large logo livery on a very wet day in Glasgow Central station. She is at the head of a Mk 3 InterCity rake, including a new Driving Van Trailer (DVT), and is getting ready to depart from Platform 1. It is likely there would have been an electric locomotive at the rear of the train and the reason for a Class 47 hauling the train would be a diversion via the non-electrified Glasgow South Western Line to Carlisle. This would be due to engineering works on the WCML and was the normal diversion route south. She carries the unofficial Tinsley depot name *Mentor*, which she carried between January 1991 and 1993, at which time she was renamed *Resounding*. She was new in September 1964 as No. D1622 and was later renumbered 47041 before becoming No. 47630 in November 1985. She would later be renumbered yet again in June 1994, becoming No. 47764 after being fitted with long-range fuel tanks. By April 2001 she had been withdrawn and spent time stored at Wigan Springs Branch component recovery depot. She was finally scrapped in August 2005 by EMR Kingsbury.

Class 47 Locomotive No. 47642

New to traffic in September 1964 as No. D1621 following construction at BR Crewe works, No. 47642 is pictured in the yard at BRML Springburn, Glasgow. She is wearing old InterCity livery with Scotrail branding and has also been fitted with the Highland Rail Stag logo. Many Scottish-allocated locomotives carried this logo over the years including some recent Class 66 locomotives. She carried the name *Strathisla* between 1986 and 1992. She has carried a few fleetnumbers over the years: No. 47040 from 1973 to 1986; No. 47642 from 1986 to 1994; and finally No. 47766 from 1994. She received Rail Express System livery in 1992 and received the name *Resolute* shortly after. After a period of storage at Toton depot she was scrapped by Harry Needle Railroad Co. on-site at Toton in July 2004.

Class 47 Locomotive No. 47671

This locomotive has carried no less than five fleetnumbers and two names over the years. She was constructed in December 1965 at Brush, Loughborough, and entered service shortly after, numbered D1925. In 1973 she received the number 47248 and in 1984 she became No. 47616. In 1991 she became one of six Class 47/4 locomotives based at Inverness depot to have their ETH index increased from sixty-six to seventy-five. The six locomotives received numbers from 47671 to 47677. Finally, in January 1995, she was renumbered once again to become No. 47789. The first name she carried was *Y Ddraig Goch/The Red Dragon* even when based at Inverness. Later she carried the name *Lindisfarne*. She is pictured wearing BR Blue Large logo livery at Edinburgh Waverley station getting ready to depart with a rake of Mk 1 InterCity-liveried coaches. By 2004 she was in storage at Toton depot and is recorded as being scrapped by EMR Kingsbury in May 2007.

Class 47 Locomotive No. 47672

Another of the six Inverness Class 47/4 locomotives with increased ETH index, No. 47672 is pictured in BR Mainline livery at Inverness station. New in September 1964 as No. D1617, she was one of many Class 47 locomotives constructed at BR Crewe works. After the 1973 TOPS renumbering she received fleetnumber 47036, followed by No. 47562 a few years later. In July 1991 she received the number 47672, which she carried until March 1993. She then reverted to No. 47562 briefly before receiving the number 47760 after conversion to a Class 47/7 locomotive in March 1994. She has carried three nameplates over the years. Between 1983 and 1991 she was named *Sir William Burrell*, and in 1993 she was named *Restless* before receiving the name *Ribblehead Viaduct* in 1999. Happily, No. 47760 lives on and is an active member of the West Coast Railway's fleet, currently wearing the company's maroon livery.

Class 47 Locomotive No. 47677

No. 47677 is pictured at Platform 10 of Glasgow's Central station. She is wearing InterCity livery with a train formed of matching Mk 2 coaches. She was the last of the six Inverness-based Class 47/4 locomotives with an increased ETH index. The increased ETH index would allow these locomotives to provide enough power to sleeper coaches when operating sleeper services. The final two locomotives, No. 47676 and No. 47677, were later fitted with high phosphorous brake blocks, which restricted their top speed to 75 mph. No. 47677 was new in May 1964 as No. D1742 and she received her TOPS number, 47149, in December 1973. In 1984 she was renumbered to 47617 before finally becoming No. 47677 in July 1991. For many years she carried the name *University of Stirling* and is recorded as being withdrawn from service in January 1998. No. 47677 was scrapped by Booths of Rotherham in February 1998.

Class 47 Locomotive No. 47701

In 1979 British Rail decided to convert and upgrade twelve Class 47/4 locomotives to replace the Class 27 locomotives that were employed on the Glasgow to Edinburgh express services. The twelve Class 47/4 locomotives all received long-range fuel tanks, TDM push-pull equipment and were uprated for 100 mph running. They were renumbered as Class 47/7 locomotives, receiving numbers from 47701 to 47712 and also names associated with Scotland. No. 47701 was constructed in February 1966 by Brush, Loughborough. She entered service shortly after, numbered D1932. Before becoming No. 47701, she also carried fleetnumber 47493. No. 47701 is pictured in Scotrail livery upon arrival into Glasgow Queen Street station and carries the name *Saint Andrew*. The locomotive is at the Edinburgh end of the train and has red tail lights on, indicating it has 'pushed' the train through from Edinburgh. Over time the Mk 3 coaches used on the Scotrail push-pull services would also receive matching Scotrail livery.

Class 47 Locomotive No. 47701

By 1989 the Class 47/7 locomotives' time on front line service in Scotland was coming to an end and they were all transferred south to Old Oak Common depot, London. No. 47701 is pictured on the turntable at Old Oak Common depot, London, shortly after transfer south from Scotland. She is still wearing Scotrail livery but has had her Scotrail logos and *Saint Andrew* nameplates removed. Over the years she has carried three names: *Saint Andrew; Old Oak Common Traction and Rolling Stock Depot*; and finally *Waverley*. No. 47701 lives on and after some time with Fragonset Railways is now owned by Nemesis Rail, and is currently being operated on the Dartmoor preserved railway wearing a two-tone green livery.

Class 47 Locomotive No. 47702

New to traffic in July 1966 as No. D1947 following construction by Brush, Loughborough, No. 47702 was also No. 47504 between 1973 and 1979. She is pictured receiving an overhaul and repaint into Network SouthEast livery during 1990 at BRML Springburn, Glasgow. After release from BRML Springburn, she could be found on her usual duties operating push-pull services with Scotrail, wearing full Network SouthEast livery. This would not be the last repaint for this locomotive, as by 1996 she was wearing Railfreight livery followed by Virgin Trains livery by 1998. She carried two names over the years: *Saint Cuthbert* between 1979 and 1994, followed by *County of Suffolk* from 1994. She was withdrawn in April 2000 and spent almost five years stored before being scrapped on-site at Toton depot by Harry Needle Railroad Co.

Class 47 Locomotive No. 47706

No. 47706 is pictured approaching London Paddington station running light engine. While No. 47702 was operating in Scotland in full Network SouthEast livery, No. 47706 was operating in London in full Scotrail livery! No. 47706 never did receive a repaint following her time in Scotland and when scrapped at Crewe works in August 1995 by MRJ Phillips, she was still wearing Scotrail livery. She was the first of the Class 47/7 to lose her Scottish name, *Strathclyde*, in 1986. However, in this photograph she still carries her Scotrail logos and Terrier dog emblem. She was new in service as No. D1936 in March 1966 and went on to carry fleetnumber 47494 before conversion to a Class 47/7.

Class 47 Locomotive No. 47707

No. 47707 was constructed by Brush, Loughborough, in August 1966 and entered service as No. D1949. She went on to carry fleetnumber 47506 before conversion in 1979 to become a Class 47/7 numbered 47707. She carried the name *Holyrood* between 1979 and 1996. No. 47707 is pictured in 1991 wearing Network SouthEast livery at Old Oak Common depot, London, while undergoing electrical testing. She would later transfer to the Parcels sector and by 1994 was wearing Rail Express Systems livery. In August 1996 she was stored at Crewe following the introduction of new Class 325 Parcel EMU trains. After spending many years stored at Crewe, she was purchased and moved to Barrowhill depot, where she remained in storage for a further few years. No. 47707 was the locomotive that was propelling the 17.30 Edinburgh to Glasgow service that collided with a cow near Polmont in July 1984. The accident raised concerns at the time about push-pull operations with the locomotive at the rear of the train. The end of the line for No. 47707 came in February 2010 when she was scrapped by Booths of Rotherham.

Class 47 Locomotive No. 47708

No. 47708 is pictured on the turntable at Old Oak Common depot, London, in 1991, having recently been named *Templecombe*. She is looking smart in freshly painted Network SouthEast livery, including white lining on her wheels. She was constructed at Crewe works in October 1965 and entered service as No. D1968 shortly after. She would later carry fleetnumber 47516 before conversion to a Class 47/7, at which point she received fleetnumber 47708. Between June 1979 and October 1990, she carried the name *Waverley*. She was withdrawn in May 1993 following a mechanical failure and spent two years in storage at Crewe, close to where she was constructed twenty-eight years earlier. She was scrapped in August 1995 on-site at Crewe, still wearing Network SouthEast livery.

Class 47 Locomotive No. 47803

New to traffic as No. D1956 she was constructed at Brush, Loughborough, in December 1966. She later became No. 47260 in 1974, followed by No. 47553 in September 1974 and then finally No. 47803 in March 1989. Between 1989 and 1992 she carried the name *Woman's Guild*. She is pictured in original InterCity livery at York station. In April 1993 she received a trial Infrastructure livery of yellow, grey and red stripe. It basically consisted of repainting everything above her red stripe yellow and was not the most attractive livery. Only one other locomotive, a Class 31, also received this livery. By 1998 she had been stored at Stratford depot. She later moved to Peak Rail for further storage and is recorded as being scrapped by Ron Hull, Rotherham, in February 2007, still wearing her Yellow Pearl livery.

Class 47 Locomotive No. 47807

The last of the Class 47/0 locomotives to be converted into Class 47/4s also received extended fuel tanks. To ensure they could be easily identified, all the Class 47/4 with extended fuel tanks were renumbered into Class 47/8 locomotives in 1989. No. 47807 started life in December 1964 as No. D1639 following construction at BR Crewe works. She was later renumbered 47055 in 1974, followed by No. 47562 in 1986. In July 1989 she became No. 47807. She is pictured at Manchester Victoria station looking smart in full InterCity livery. The locomotive lives on today as No. 57304. In 2002 twelve Class 47 locomotives were rebuilt as Class 57 locomotives with a further four in 2003. They were used for many years to rescue failed passenger trains or to haul electric trains over non-electrified routes. As the work for these units decreased, many were put into storage. No. 57304 is now part of the DRS active fleet and wears DRS livery. Since 1996 she has carried a number of liveries, including Porterbrook, two different Virgin Trains liveries and DRS livery. She has also carried a number of names over the years. From 1998 to 2002 she carried the name *The Lion of Vienna*, between 2002 and 2010 she was named *Gordon Tracey – Thunderbirds,* reflecting her role at the time, and finally she now carries *Pride of Cheshire*.

Class 47 Locomotive No. 47809

No. 47809 was new to traffic as No. D1640 in December 1964, following construction at BR Crewe works. In 1974 she became No. 47056, followed by No. 47654 in May 1986. She was renumbered into the 47/8 subclass in July 1989 and is pictured in full InterCity livery outside BRML Springburn, Glasgow. On 27 June 1994 she was involved in a serious accident at Morpeth wherein she became the third train since 1969 to derail after taking the tight curve too fast. Fortunately, no one was seriously injured, although the locomotive received extensive damage. She was returned to traffic in May 1994 as No. 47783, wearing Rail Express Systems livery. By 2002 she was stored at Crewe and is recorded as officially withdrawn in April 2007. She was scrapped by Ron Hull, Rotherham, in October 2007. She carried the name *Finsbury Park* between September 1986 and May 1995 and shortly after carried the name *Saint Peter*.

Class 47 Locomotive No. 47972

In 1988 four Class 47/4 locomotives were acquired by the Railway Technical Centre for Departmental duties including hauling test trains around the network. Initially they received numbers in the 97 Departmental series, but shortly after received numbers in the Class 47/9 series. No. 47972 was new as No. D1646 in December 1964, following construction at BR Crewe works. In 1974 she became No. 47062, followed by No. 47545 in December 1979. In 1988 she became No. 97545 and then finally No. 47972 in July 1989. Between 1993 and 1999 she carried the name *The Royal Army Ordnance Corps*. She is pictured wearing BR Blue large logo livery while completing a shunting movement in Sheffield station. From 1993 she carried Central Services grey and red livery. By 2002 she was in storage at Crewe depot and she later moved to West Coast Railways at Carnforth where she remained in storage. She was scrapped by Booths of Rotherham in March 2010, at which time she was still carrying Central Services livery.

Class 50 Locomotive No. 50003

The Class 50 locomotives were constructed by English Electric at Vulcan Foundry, Newton-le-Willows, between 1967 and 1968. There were fifty in total and with a power rating of 2,700 hp were known as English Electric Type 4s. They were also known as 'Hoovers' to enthusiasts due to the noise created by the cooling fans. No. 50003 was new as No. D403 in January 1968, receiving fleetnumber 50003 in 1973. In 1978 all the Class 50 locomotives were named after Royal Navy vessels and No. 50003 was named *Temeraire*. She is pictured wearing revised Network SouthEast livery at London Waterloo station. As can be seen in this photo, corrosion has set in around the cab area. Withdrawal would come shortly after this photo was taken in July 1991, with scrapping taking place at MC Metals, Glasgow, in April 1992.

Class 50 Locomotive No. 50004

A sad-looking No. 50004 wearing BR Blue large logo livery is pictured stored, awaiting her fate. She received this livery in September 1984 at Doncaster works after refurbishment to improve reliability. She was new in December 1967 as No. D404 and she received fleetnumber 50004 in December 1973. She carried the name *St Vincent* from May 1978 but has had her nameplates removed by the time this photograph was taken. She is recorded as being withdrawn in June 1990 and was scrapped at Booths, Rotherham, in May 1992.

Class 50 Locomotive No. 50015

In 1992, as the number of Class 50 locomotives in service was reducing fast, three locomotives received special liveries. No. 50015 received Dutch Departmental grey and yellow livery and attended a number of open day events. She is pictured passing through Crewe station with sister Class 50, No. 50008, which at the time wore special BR Blue livery. The Dutch livery suited these locomotives well. She was new to traffic in April 1968 as D415. She was renumbered 50015 in December 1973 and carried the name *Valiant* from April 1978. Happily, she is one of eighteen Class 50 locomotives still around. No. 50015 is preserved in BR Blue large logo livery by the Bury Valiant group and resides on the East Lancashire Railway, Bury. Strangely she is missing her nameplates in this photo, but appeared to have been refitted shortly after this photo was taken.

Class 50 Locomotive No. 50017

New to traffic as No. D417 in April 1968, she received the fleetnumber 50017 in December 1973. She was named *Royal Oak* in April 1978. She is pictured wearing revised Network SouthEast livery at Clapham Junction, London. No. 50017 is another of the Class 50 locomotives that survives to this day. She has carried a number of liveries over the years. As well as BR blue, BR Blue large logo livery and Network SouthEast livery, between 1996 and 1999 she was repainted into Railfreight General livery and carried temporary number 50117. In 2000 she was contracted to VSOE (Venice Simplon Orient Express Co.) to work the Northern Belle service between Manchester and Bath. For this she received a maroon livery in LMS style. Following this No. 50017 was stored at Tyseley depot before entering preservation on the Plym Valley Railway in 2009. She is currently operational and has been restored to original Network SouthEast livery.

Class 50 Locomotive No. 50018

The Class 50 locomotives were ordered to operate express passenger services north of Crewe on the WCML (West Coast Main Line). They were capable of 100 mph and for the first ten years were leased to BR by English Electric, before later being purchased outright. Once the electrification of the WCML was completed to Glasgow, in 1974 they were transferred to the South West of England and operated services from London Paddington and later London Waterloo. No. 50018 was new in April 1968 as No. D418. She was renumbered to 50018 in December 1973 and received the name *Resolution* in April 1978. She is pictured in revised Network SouthEast livery at the head of a train of matching coaching stock at London Waterloo station. Withdrawal came in July 1991 and she was scrapped at MC Metals, Glasgow, in July 1992.

Class 50 Locomotive No. 50021

No. 50021 entered service as D421 in May 1968. She was renumbered 50021 in December 1973 and received the name *Rodney* in July 1978. She was withdrawn in October 1990 and entered preservation in October 1992. She is pictured wearing BR Blue large logo livery during an open day event at Eastleigh depot on 27 September 1992. In the late 1990s she spent time at the Scottish Railway Preservation Society, Bo'ness, before moving to the Severn Valley Railway. During April 2017 she was undergoing restoration at Eastleigh works.

Class 50 Locomotive No. 50030

In the early 1990s, as the Class 50 locomotives were being withdrawn, an ambitious charity engineering project called Operation Collingwood was established. The idea was to train young engineering apprentices with the overall aim of rebuilding railway locomotives. No. 50030 was one of six Class 50 locomotives chosen for the project, but the project ultimately failed and was wound up in 2002. Four of the Class 50 locomotives were finally scrapped, but No. 50029 and No. 50030 survived and were sold to the Renown Repulse Restoration Group. New into traffic in July 1968 as No. D430, she received the number 50030 after the TOPS renumbering in December 1973. She was named *Repulse* in April 1978 and is recorded as being withdrawn in April 1992. Pictured looking a bit tatty at the buffers at London Waterloo station wearing revised Network SouthEast livery, No. 50030 now carries BR Blue large logo livery and is currently under restoration at Peak Rail.

Class 50 Locomotive No. 50033

No. 50033 was constructed in July 1968 and entered service shortly after, numbered D433. She became No. 50033 in December 1973 and was named *Glorious* in June 1978. No. 50033 is pictured in revised Network SouthEast livery approaching Salisbury station. She remained in service until 1994 and towards the end of her time with British Rail she could be found operating special railtours. No. 50033 then passed to the National Railway Museum at York, and was preserved in BR Blue large logo livery. In 2003 the National Railway Museum offered No. 50033 for ongoing preservation if a suitable owner could be found. After a period at the North Yorkshire Moors Railway, she moved to the Swindon Steam Railway Museum in 2004. The locomotive was moved shortly after to Tyseley depot and has been in storage there since, still wearing BR Blue large logo livery.

Class 50 Locomotive No. 50036

New to traffic as No. D436 in August 1968, she was later renumbered 50036 in December 1973. She was named *Victorious* in May 1978. She is pictured in revised Network SouthEast livery while being stripped inside Stratford depot. Officially withdrawn in April 1991, she was scrapped by Booths, Rotherham, in June 1992.

Class 50 Locomotive No. 50037

Pictured producing a fair amount of smoke at the head of a train at London Waterloo station, No. 50037 is wearing revised Network SouthEast livery. She was new as No. D437 in September 1968 and received the name *Illustrious* in June 1978. Over the years she has also carried BR Blue livery, BR Blue large logo livery and original Network SouthEast livery. No. 50037 was withdrawn in September 1991. Part of her still remains and although she was scrapped by MC Metals, Springburn, Glasgow, in December 1992, both her cabs were retained and are now stored at Peak Rail as spares for No. 50029 and No. 50030.

Class 50 Locomotive No. 50048

No. 50048 was constructed in December 1968 and entered service as No. D448 shortly after. In 1973 she received fleetnumber 50048 and was named *Dauntless* in March 1978. She is pictured at Salisbury station wearing revised Network SouthEast livery. She has also carried BR blue, BR Blue large logo and original Network SouthEast livery. She is recorded as being withdrawn in July 1991 and was scrapped at MC Metals, Springburn, Glasgow, in April 1992.

Class 50 Locomotive No. D400

New into service as No. D400 in October 1967 after construction at Vulcan Foundry, Newton-le-Willows, she received fleetnumber 50050 in February 1974. She was named *Fearless* in August 1978 and went on to receive BR Blue large logo livery, followed by Network SouthEast livery. By 1992 only eight members of the fleet remained in traffic. Three of the remaining Class 50 locomotives, Nos 50008, 50015 and 50050, all gained special liveries. *Rail Magazine* managed to raise funds to return No. 50050 to BR Blue as No. D400. She completed a number of main line tours including on the northern end of the WCML as No. D400. She is recorded as being withdrawn from BR service in 1994. However, she is now preserved still in BR Blue livery as No. D400. She is owned by Boden Rail Engineering and is main line certified. No. D400, which was unnamed at the time, is pictured approaching London Waterloo station hauling a train of Network SouthEast coaches.

Class 55 Locomotive No. 55015

English Electric built twenty-two Class 55 locomotives between 1961 and 1962. They were fitted with two Napier 1,650 hp engines and were capable of 100 mph. They were known as Deltics due to the Delta configuration of pistons and originally operated flagship services on the East Coast Main Line, being allocated to three depots: Finsbury Park, Gateshead, and Haymarket. When the HST trains were introduced in 1978, the Deltics were relegated to secondary duties, with the fleet being withdrawn by 1981. Six of the twenty-two locomotives were later preserved, including No. 55015, which is pictured here in BR Blue livery attending an open day event at Manchester Longsight depot on 20 April 1992. The white cab window surrounds signify that the locomotive was allocated to Finsbury Park depot. No. 55015 is now resident at Barrow Hill depot and is currently undergoing overhaul, carrying two-tone green livery. She was named *Tulyar* from new and her current owner is recorded as the Deltic Preservation Society.

Class 56 Locomotive No. 56003

The Class 56, also known as a Brush Type 5 locomotive, was built between 1976 and 1984. A total of 135 locomotives were built, all being fitted with 3,250 hp Ruston Paxman engines, and all were designed for heavy freight work. Although based on the Class 47 body shell and designed by Brush at Falcon works, Loughborough, due to capacity problems the first thirty locomotives were built in Romania by Electroputere of Craiova. Later examples were built at BREL Doncaster and BREL Crewe works. No. 56003 is pictured in Railfreight livery with No. 58047, passing Worksop depot on 1 September 1991 during an open day event. No. 56003 was withdrawn in February 2004 and after a brief spell in preservation she returned to service in 2008 as No. 56312. She is now operated by BARS (British American Railway Services), who are a British locomotive spot hire company. She carried the name *Artemis* between 2008 and 2012, followed by *Jeremiah Dixon (Son of Country Durham, Surveyor of the Mason–Dixon Line USA)* in 2013.

Class 56 Locomotive No. 56020

Another of the Romanian-built Class 56 locomotives, No. 56020 is pictured at Doncaster station in BR Blue livery. In the background, a 1986 Mk 2 Ford Fiesta can be seen – a very common sight on the UK streets at the time. In 1987 this was the second top selling car in the UK with 150,000 sales, the number one top selling vehicle being the Ford Escort. No. 56020 entered service in May 1977 and is recorded as withdrawn twenty years later in June 1997. She was scrapped by Booths of Rotherham in January 1998.

Class 56 Locomotive No. 56022

No. 56022 was constructed by Electroputere, Romania, in May 1977. She is pictured wearing BR Blue livery while hauling a MGR coal train through Crewe station. By 1994 she carried Railfreight livery and later received Transrail livery. By 2008 she had moved to Wolsingham on the Weardale Railway. She would spend four years stored here before being scrapped by EMR Kingsbury in February 2012.

Class 56 Locomotives Nos 56039, 56052 and 56041

Three members of the Class 56 fleet gather around the turntable at Old Oak Common depot, London, wearing Railfreight Construction livery. All three locomotives were built at BREL Doncaster works. No. 56039 entered service in February 1978. She entered service in BR Blue livery and would go on to receive Railfreight, Railfreight Construction and Loadhaul livery before being withdrawn in January 2004. She was scrapped by TJ Thomson, Stockton-on-Tees, shortly afterwards. Between 1994 and 1997 she carried the name *ABP Port of Hull*.

Class 56 Locomotive No. 56041

No. 56041 was constructed at BREL Doncaster works in February 1978 and is pictured in Railfreight Construction livery at Old Oak Common depot London. She later received all-over pale grey livery while new owners EWS Railways decided what livery to adopt. In time she received standard EWS maroon and yellow livery but was stored at Healey Mills, Wakefield, in April 2005. After many years in storage she was officially withdrawn in July 2010 and was scrapped by EMR Attercliffe in January 2011.

Class 56 Locomotive No. 56052

In 1995 Canadian train operator Wisconsin Central formed a UK Freight company called EWS (English, Welsh & Scottish) Railways. Between 1995 and 1996 they acquired five of the six UK rail freight operators. Shortly afterwards EWS placed an order for 250 Class 66 locomotives. The first locomotives were delivered to the UK in June 1998. The influx of newer locomotives resulted in the withdrawal and storage of many older locomotives including many Class 56 locomotives. No. 56052 was constructed at BREL Doncaster works in December 1978. She is pictured easing onto the turntable at Old Oak Common depot, London, wearing Railfreight Construction livery. In May 1997 she received the name *The Cardiff Rod Mill*. By 2002 she had been stored at Immingham depot where she would remain until she was scrapped by Booths of Rotherham in April 2009.

Class 56 Locomotive No. 56065

The official name for Class 56 locomotives was Brush Type 5. However, they were known to enthusiasts as 'Grids' due to the grid like cover fitted on the front of the locomotives to cover the warning horns. locomotives numbered from 56056 to 56135 had a larger, more noticeable 'grid' on the front as can be seen on this photograph of No. 56065. She is pictured wearing original Railfreight grey red stripe livery passing through Doncaster station with a MGR coal train. In the background, outside BREL Doncaster works, can be seen a new InterCity Mk 4 DVT and Mk 4 coach. After a period of storage, she was one of twenty-six Class 56 locomotives that would be hired by Fertis in 2004 for work in France to construct a new high-speed rail line. All twenty-six locomotives received Fertis grey livery in the UK prior to dispatch to France. Upon return to the UK a few years later, she returned to storage at Crewe, and then Burton-on-Trent. She is now owned by UK Rail Leasing Ltd and remains in storage at Leicester, still wearing its Fertis livery.

Class 56 Locomotive No. 56072

New to traffic as No. 56072 in January 1980 after construction at BREL Doncaster works, she is pictured undergoing maintenance at Toton depot and can be seen in the main shed in the company of a Class 60 and two Class 58 locomotives. She is wearing Railfreight Coal livery and would go on to receive Transrail livery. By 2007 she had been stored with many other Class 56 at Healey Mills, Wakefield. She was scrapped in October 2010 by EMR Attercliffe.

Class 56 Locomotive No. 56091

No. 56091 was constructed at the BREL works in Doncaster in June 1981. Between 1988 and 1997 she was named *Castle Donington Power Station*. In 1998 she received EWS maroon and yellow livery and was named *Stanton*. She is pictured at Manchester Victoria station while operating a charter train. She was one of the twenty-six Class 56 locomotives to be hired by Fertis rail to operate construction trains in France. Prior to leaving for France she received Fertis grey livery. After return to the UK she was sold to BARS (British American Railway Services), who are a British locomotive spot-hire company. She is currently stored in Fertis grey livery with power unit issues.

Class 56 Locomotive No. 56122

The final twenty Class 56 locomotives were built at BREL Crewe works rather than BREL Doncaster. The reason for this switch was to allow BREL Doncaster to construct the Class 58 locomotives. No. 56122 was new in July 1983 and had a very short career, being withdrawn after just nine years. She was withdrawn in October 1992 following front-end collision damage and was scrapped in November 1995 by Booths of Rotherham. She carried the name *Wilton – Coalpower* from April 1988 until withdrawal. She is pictured at the rear of Toton depot shortly after withdrawal and has already been partially cannibalised. The end that received the damage is closest to the shed. In the background can be seen a Class 20 locomotive and a Class 60 locomotive just inside the shed.

Class 58 Locomotive No. 58013

The last locomotives to be built at BREL Doncaster works were the Class 58 locomotives. Fifty locomotives were constructed between 1983 and 1987 and all entered service in original Railfreight grey, red stripe livery. They were known as BREL Type 5 locomotives and featured a new modular construction method. BR had hoped for some export orders but none were placed. In later life many Class 58 locomotives did get exported and saw further service in Spain, the Netherlands and France. No. 58013 was new in March 1984. On 6 August 1987 she was involved in a derailment at Baddesley, Warwickshire. By 1996 she had been repainted in Mainline Freight blue livery. All Class 58 locomotives were withdrawn by 2002. No. 58013 spent many years in storage with many other Class 58 locomotives at Eastleigh depot. She was later sold to ETF for further service in France. No. 58013 is pictured in Railfreight Coal livery, taking part in an open day event at Worksop depot on 1 September 1991.

Class 58 Locomotive No. 58038 and No. 58032

Two Class 58 locomotives, Nos 58038 and 58032, are pictured wearing Railfreight Coal livery at Toton depot in the company of No. 47306 and No. 60006. All fifty Class 58 locomotives were allocated to Toton depot. After being placed into storage for many years, No. 58038 was hired to ACTS for service in the Netherlands. Upon completion of work in the Netherlands she then moved to France, where she saw further service with ETF. No. 58032 has also operated in France. Between October 2004 and December 2006 she was hired by Fertis. She would later return to France and saw further service with ETF. No. 58032 was named *Thoresby Colliery* in October 1995.

Class 58 Locomotive No. 58039

Pictured at BRML Doncaster open day event on 12 July 1992, No. 58039 is wearing Railfreight Coal livery. She was constructed at Doncaster in March 1986. Between 1986 and 1997 she carried the name *Rugeley Power Station*. She would go on to receive EWS maroon and yellow livery before being stored with the rest of the Class 58 fleet. No. 58039 was another Class 58 that saw further service with both ACTS in the Netherlands and ETF in France.

Class 59 Locomotive No. 59001

In 1983, aggregates company Foster Yeoman investigated what cost savings could be made if it owned its own locomotives. The company already owned its own wagons and invitations to tender were issued. The company demanded a 95 per cent availability with the power to haul heavy loaded trains with one locomotive. Although tenders were received from BREL (Class 58) and Brush (Class 60), only General Motors (GM) were prepared to guarantee availability of 95 per cent. This would mean Foster Yeoman would only require four GM locomotives rather than eleven UK-built locomotives. An order was placed with GM and the four locomotives were constructed in 1985 at La Grange, Illinois, USA. They arrived at Southampton on the MV *Fairlift*, which docked on 21 January 1986. They all entered service the following month. Known as General Motors Type 5 locomotives, they were fitted with a General Motors 645E3C two-stroke engine capable of 3,300 hp. During a test run, No. 59002 was able to haul forty 100-ton wagons up a 1 in 25 gradient on curved, damp track. In June 1986 she received the name *Yeoman Endeavour*. She is pictured at Tinsley depot, Sheffield, while attending an open day event on 29 September 1990. Due to increased contracts, a fifth Class 59 was ordered in 1989. The locomotive is now owned by Mendip Rail, who own all five Class 59/0 and all four Class 59/1 locomotives. The company has a depot at Merehead.

Class 59 Locomotive No. 59102

Following the success of the first five Class 59 locomotives, ARC Ltd placed an order for four Class 59 locomotives for delivery in 1990. These were designated Class 59/1 and were very similar in appearance. The Class 59/1 locomotives were later fitted with yaw dampers, which increased their permitted top speed from 60 mph to 75 mph. All four locomotives arrived on the MV *Stellamare*, which docked in the UK on 20 October 1990. They all entered service on 11 November 1990. The final batch of Class 59 locomotives for the UK were six Class 59/2 locomotives ordered by National Power in 1994 for MGR coal work. All Class 59/0 and Class 59/1 locomotives are now owned by Mendip Rail. This was a company formed by Yeoman Foster and Hanson (formally ARC), and has now obtained train-operating company status. The Class 59/0 and Class 59/1 locomotives now operate in a common pool but are still owned by their parent companies. In April 1998 EWS railways took over National Power's rail operations and the Class 59/2 locomotives passed to EWS. The Class 59 locomotives were the forerunners of the hugely successful Class 66 locomotives, which were also constructed by General Motors. There are now over 450 Class 66 locomotives based in the UK. No. 59102 is pictured at Ashford Chart Leacon depot on 6 June 1992, taking part in an open day event. She was named *Village of Chantry* in September 1991.

Class 60 Locomotive No. 60001

In August 1987, British Rail invited tenders for 100 heavy-haul Type 5 locomotives. Tenders had to be submitted by November 1987 and three companies – Metro-Cammell, GEC/GM and Brush – duly submitted tenders. In the end Brush won the contract, worth £1.2 million per locomotive, with the locomotives being known as Brush Type 5s. The first locomotive was delivered on time in June 1989, just thirteen months after the contract was signed. It would, however, be almost two years before No. 60001 completed testing and was finally accepted into traffic. No. 60001 is pictured at the rear of Polmadie depot in Glasgow. The author worked here at the time this photo was taken and around this time both No. 60001 and No. 60005 were stabled here for crew training. Between August 1991 and September 1996 she carried the name *Steadfast*, and between February 2001 and May 2014 she was named *The Railway Observer*. No. 60001 is wearing Railfreight Construction livery and would go on to receive EWS maroon and yellow livery, followed by DB livery in 2013. She was stored in 2006 for six years with a defective engine but is happily once again an active member of the DB Railways fleet.

Class 60 Locomotive No. 60005

The other member of the Class 60 fleet that could often be found at Polmadie depot for crew training was No. 60005. She is pictured at the rear of Polmadie depot and again wears Railfreight construction livery. The Class 60 locomotives were fitted with eight-cylinder, 145 litre Mirrlees Blackstone 8MB275T engines, which were considered to be one of the most fuel efficient engines at the time. The engine was a higher-powered version of the Mirrlees engines that had been fitted as a trial to Nos 37901–37904 in 1986. The Class 60 locomotives eventually settled down to become very reliable engines. However, for the first few years the new Class 60s experienced many problems and numerus modifications had to be carried out before they were all accepted into traffic. No. 60005 was new to traffic in April 1991. She carried the name *Skiddaw* between April 1991 and November 1997, while between April 2000 and July 2009 she was named *BP Gas Avonmouth*. All Class 60 locomotives passed to EWS Railways and most have now spent many years in storage. No. 60005 is one locomotive that has been stored for many years at Toton depot and was one of twenty Class 60 locomotives offered for sale by DB Railways in August 2016.

Class 60 Locomotive No. 60006

No. 60006 is pictured at Toton depot not long after delivery from Brush. She was new in April 1990 and between 1990 and June 1997 she carried the name *Great Gable*. In July 1997 she received the name *Scunthorpe Ironmaster*. She took pride of place at an open day event at Toton depot on 30 August 1998, resplendent in a blue livery for Corus Steel and later, around 2003, received a second Corus livery, this time silver. She was withdrawn from service in September 2010 and has been stored at Toton depot ever since. She was one of twenty Class 60 locomotives offered for sale by DB Railways in August 2016.

Class 60 Locomotive No. 60046

New into service in April 1991, No. 60046 received the name *William Wilberforce* shortly after. She is pictured in Railfreight Coal livery receiving fuel between freight duties. Like many Class 60 locomotives, she has spent years in storage. No. 60046, now devoid of her nameplates, is currently stored at Crewe depot wearing Railfreight livery with large EWS logos. The run-down of the Class 60 fleet started in 2003 when many of the fleet were stored. By 2007 only approximately fifty of the fleet would be found in service and by 2009 only fifteen were available for use. In 2010 DB Railways, the new owners of EWS Railways, announced that twenty Class 60 locomotives would be overhauled. This began with seven locomotives in January 2011 and over the next two years approximately eighteen locomotives received overhaul and upgrade, which DB Railways referred to as 'Super Class 60s'. Freight operator Colas Rail purchased ten Class 60 locomotives in 2014 and they can be found working for Colas around the country in Colas's black, orange and yellow livery.

Class 60 Locomotive No. 60049

No. 60049 was new to traffic in May 1991. She carried the name *Scafell* between May 1991 and November 1996. She is pictured at Thornaby depot on 20 September 1992 while attending an open day event. She is wearing Railfreight Metals livery and over time would pass to EWS Railways and receive EWS maroon and yellow livery. After a few years in storage, she returned to service, and saw much use around the West Country between around 2012 until February 2016, when she was again stored at Toton depot. All the Class 60 locomotives were named from new. Those allocated to the Construction and Metals sectors received names of British mountains. Some Coal sector locomotives also received names of mountains, while others and those from the Petroleum sector were named after famous British citizens. Two locomotives were the exceptions: No. 60001 was named *Steadfast* and No. 60098 was named *Charles Francis Brush* after the inventor born in 1849 that would go on to form the Brush company in 1880.

Class 60 Locomotive No. 60077

Pictured in Railfreight Coal livery, No. 60077 can be seen in the company of three other Class 60 locomotives at Toton depot. She would later receive Mainline Freight branding, followed by EWS branding, in place of her Coal subsector logos. She received the name *Canisp* following entry into service in November 1991. No. 60077 has spent many years in storage alongside many of her sisters at Toton depot.

Class 101 No. 101076 Vehicle No. 51224

The Class 101 Diesel Multiple Unit (DMU) was one of the most successful and longest serving first generation DMUs. They were constructed by Metro-Cammell at Washwood Heath, Birmingham, between 1956 and 1959. Class 101 units could be seen throughout the country and, remarkably, the last unit was not withdrawn until 2003, when it was forty-seven years old. No. T076 is pictured at Manchester Piccadilly station wearing Strathclyde PTE orange and black livery. She had recently been transferred down to Tyseley depot from Eastfield depot in Glasgow, where she was previously formed as a three-car unit and numbered 101304. She would later be refurbished, receiving Regional Railways livery and becoming No. 101679. She is recorded as still being in active service as late as June 1998.

Class 101 No. 101691 Vehicle No. 51253

Newly refurbished and repainted into Regional Railways livery, No. 101691 is pictured in 1993 awaiting her next duty within a smoke-filled Edinburgh Waverley station. By 1997 she had lost her middle coach to become a two-car unit and she had also been repainted into Strathclyde PTE orange and black livery. In 2000 she was transferred to Longsight depot, Manchester, where she operated in her Strathclyde livery until 2003. She was stripped by enthusiasts for spare parts at the Caerwent Royal Navy propellant factory in January 2004.

Class 101 No. 101106 Vehicle No. 53139

Pictured at Ilford depot near London, No. 101106 is pictured in BR blue and grey livery. At the time, the unit was allocated to Norwich depot. The leading vehicle is No. 53139 and she was constructed in 1956. The large antenna on the front of the unit is for the RETB (Radio Electronic Token Block) radio signalling system, which was in use on the East Suffolk line until 2012.

Class 101 Observation Car No. 6300

New in 1958 as No. 56356, she was later renumbered to 54356. In 1987 she was one of two Class 101 DTCL vehicles to be converted into observation cars. Upon conversion she was named *Hebridean* and received fleetnumber 6300. She was used extensively on the Inverness to Kyle of Lochalsh services. She is pictured at BRML Springburn, Glasgow. She was withdrawn in 1994 and was purchased a few years later for preservation. In August 2013 she was recorded as being owned by the Barry Tourist Railway and had been stored in a poor condition for many years.

Class 101 Unknown Number

A two-car Class 101 is pictured at Doncaster station, freshly outshopped in Regional Railways livery. I always thought that this livery suited the Class 101 units well. Each Class 101 vehicle was fitted with two 150 hp Leyland or AEC engines. Although all have now been withdrawn from service, forty-one Class 101 vehicles have been preserved.

Class 107 No. 101030 Vehicle No. 52030

The Class 107 units were constructed by BR Derby works in 1960 and were known as Derby 'Heavyweights' since they were constructed of steel. A fleet of seventy-eight vehicles were constructed and these were formed into twenty-six sets. They were originally numbered as sets 107425–107449. When the Class 156 units were due to be delivered, the Class 107 sets were renumbered in 1988 to 107725–107749. They were renumbered again in 1990 when the Class 158 units were due to be delivered. This time they received set numbers 107025–107049. No. 107030 is pictured in the yard outside BRML Springburn, Glasgow, and despite being over thirty years old when this picture was taken, still looks smart in her Strathclyde SPT livery. Most of the Class 107 units were all withdrawn from public service by 1991. Some units saw further service in the Departmental fleet, including both driving coaches from 107030, which became a sandite unit based at Haymarket depot. The leading coach in this picture, No. 52030, was renumbered 977831 during her time as a sandite vehicle. She is one of eleven Class 107 vehicles preserved and is currently under restoration at the Strathspey Railway, Aviemore.

Class 107 No. 101745 Vehicle No. 52015

The Class 107 units were always based in Scotland and operated over most of the diesel routes from Glasgow Central station. This included the line to Kilmacolm, where the author lived, before the line was closed in January 1983. No. 107745 is pictured wearing Strathclyde PTE livery while getting ready to depart from Glasgow Queen Street station. This set would go on to be renumbered set 107045 and is recorded in service as late as February 1992.

Class 108 No. CH351 Vehicle Unknown

Between 1958 and 1961, over 330 Class 108 vehicles were produced by BR Derby. Although similar in appearance to the Class 107 units, the Class 108 units were known as Derby 'Lightweights' and since they were not of all-steel construction, each coach was approximately 6 tons lighter. Withdrawal of the fleet began in 1990 with the introduction of second generation 'Sprinter' units and the final Class 108 units were withdrawn in 1993. Many Class 108 units went on to be preserved – no doubt helped by the fact they did not contain asbestos. Class 108 No. CH351 is pictured in BR blue and grey livery and presumably had been withdrawn when this photo was taken, as she is missing a number of doors. The 'CH' prefix was for Chester depot and she also wears a Welsh Dragon logo. With scotches under her rear bogie and a tail lamp fitted, it would appear she is awaiting collection for disposal.

Class 114 No. CA913 Vehicle No. 55931

Another class of first generation DMUs constructed at BR Derby were the Class 114 units. Between 1956 and 1957, 100 vehicles were constructed and formed into fifty sets. In 1960 their original 150 hp engines were replaced with 230 hp engines, which gave a much more acceptable performance. Withdrawal of the units began in the late 1980s, and by 1992 only two sets remained in service. In 1988, five Class 114 units were rebuilt as parcel DMUs. They were all repainted into Royal Mail livery and received roller shutter doors. They were renumbered and based at Cambridge depot. Their conversion would be short-lived and all would be withdrawn by 1991. Class 114 No. CA913 is pictured at BRML Springburn, Glasgow, during her time as a parcels unit. The leading vehicle is No. 55931, which was originally numbered 50040, followed by No. 53040. The set numbers were not carried on the front of these converted units.

Class 117 No. L403 Vehicle No. 51378

The Class 117 units were built by Pressed Steel Co. between 1959 and 1961. In total 123 vehicles were constructed, which were formed into forty-two sets with thirty-nine centre coaches. They were known as 'Pressed Steel Suburban' units and started life on the Western region. Set No. L403, with vehicle No. 51378 leading, is pictured looking smart in Network SouthEast livery at London Paddington station. This was a location she could often be found in until the arrival of the Class 165 Network Turbo units in 1991. By 1993 she was No. L708 and is recorded as surviving until 1997. Twelve Class 117 units would eventually be preserved.

Class 121 No. L127 Vehicle No. 55027

The Class 121 units were also constructed by Pressed Steel Co. in 1960. Sixteen single-car units were build and they were often attached to un-powered trailer units. The Class 121 was the longest serving first generation DMU, with the final vehicles being withdrawn in 2017. No. L127 is pictured in Network SouthEast livery at London Paddington station while getting ready to depart for Reading. In 1998 she received Silverlink purple, green and white livery and was named *Bletchley TMD* after her home depot. She would later enter the Departmental fleet in 2002, renumbered to 977975. She carried set number 960302 and was heavily modified for a new role as the Severn Tunnel emergency train. For this role she received Network Rail all-over yellow livery. After a few years in storage at Cardiff Canton depot, she has now entered preservation. She was initially purchased in January 2014 by the Barry Tourist Railway before moving on to the Ecclesbourne Valley Railway in June 2014.

Class 141 No. 141118 Vehicle No. 55518

The Class 141 units were the first production second generation DMUs and the first of the Pacer-type trains. Forty vehicles were produced by British Leyland in 1984, which were formed into two-car sets. The Class 141 units were very unreliable when first introduced and during 1988 they all underwent modifications at Hunslet Barclay, Kilmarnock. Part of the modifications was to change the buckeye coupler to a BSI coupler, which would then make the Class 141 units compatible with other members of the Pacer and Sprinter fleets. After the units were modified they were renumbered as Class 141/1 units. No. 141118 was originally No. 141017 prior to modifications. In 1996, No. 141118 was withdrawn and was converted to become a weedkilling train for Serco. During this time, she carried the name *Flower*. In 2002 twelve Class 141 units, including No. 141118, were sold to the Islamic Republic of Iran Railway, where they saw a few more years in service. Two units were also exported to the Netherlands and three units have now been preserved. No. 141118 is pictured wearing West Yorkshire PTE livery within York station.

Class 142 No. 142015 Vehicle No. 55556

The next batch of Pacer-type units to enter service were the Class 142 units. Ninety-six two-car Class 142 units were constructed at BREL Derby works during 1985 and 1986. The units were based on the Leyland National bus, which was a very popular vehicle at the time. The first fourteen units entered service at Newton Heath depot, Manchester, in spring 1985. They were painted in Greater Manchester orange and brown livery. The next batch of thirteen, including No. 142015, entered service at Laira depot, Plymouth, and were painted in GWR chocolate and cream livery. They were marketed as 'Skippers' and were intended for use on the branch line services around Devon and Cornwall. However, not having bogies caused terrible wheel squeal and wear to the wheel flanges, so after around three years of service they were transferred north to Manchester and Newcastle. No. 142015 is pictured at Preston station still wearing her GWR chocolate and cream livery.

Class 142 No. 142061 Vehicle No. 55711

The first fifty Class 142 units were designated Class 142/0. The next forty-six ordered in October 1985 were designated Class 142/1 units. All of the Class 142/1 units were delivered in Provincial two-tone blue livery with white stripe and initially based at either Newton Heath depot, Manchester, or Neville Hill depot, Leeds. No. 142061 is pictured at Wigan North Western station, awaiting her next duty. Only two Class 142 units have been withdrawn from service so far; however, all are due to be withdrawn between November 2018 and October 2019 as they do not comply with regulations due to be introduced in 2020 concerning accessibility.

Class 143 No. 143609 Vehicle Unknown

Twenty-five Class 143 Pacer units were to be built next. They were constructed by Hunslet Barclay, Kilmarnock, between 1985 and 1986, using a bus-style body built by Walter Alexander's of Falkirk. They all initially entered service in the North East of England, being based at Heaton depot, Newcastle. Due to problems with the SCG gearboxes fitted from new, the gearboxes were changed to Voith gearboxes. In 1989 the units that had been converted to Voith transmission were renumbered from Class 143/0 to Class 143/6 units. Between 1992 and 1993, the Class 143 fleet was transferred from Heaton depot to Cardiff Canton depot. No. 143609 is pictured wearing Regional Railways livery at Cardiff Central station, heading for Penarth. She would later carry the name *Sir Tom Jones*. Twenty-three of the initial twenty-five units built are still in service, with the other two – Nos 143613 and 143615 – being withdrawn with fire damage in 2004 and 2005. Like the Class 142 units, unless the Class 143 units receive accessibility modifications they will have to be withdrawn by the end of 2019. There are no current plans to bring any Class 143 units up to meet these standards.

Class 144 No. 144017 Vehicle Unknown

Similar in appearance to the Class 143 Pacer units, the Class 144 units were again constructed using a Walter Alexander bus body, but this time utilised a BREL underframe. Twenty-three units were constructed at Derby in 1986. The first thirteen units are two-car units, with the final ten receiving a centre car, making them three-car units, in 1987. These final ten units are the only three-car Pacer units. They all entered service in West Yorkshire PTE livery and saw extensive service in the Leeds, York and Huddersfield areas. No. 144017 is pictured a long way from her Leeds home inside Hunslet Barclay's Kilmarnock workshops. In the background can be seen a Glasgow subway vehicle and a Class 155 unit awaiting conversion into a Class 153 unit.

Class 144 No. 144018 Vehicle No. 55818

Another three-car Class 144 unit, No. 144018 is pictured wearing West Yorkshire PTE livery at York station. The future of the Class 144 units is not looking good as unless they receive accessibility modifications to bring them up to new standards due to be introduced in 2020, they will have to be withdrawn. One unit, No. 144012, was heavily refurbished in 2015 to demonstrate that it would be possible to bring the Class 144 units up to the required standard. Designated Class 144e (Evolution), the refurbished unit featured Wi-Fi, two wheelchair spaces, a fully accessible toilet, improved space for luggage and bikes, and improved 2+2 seating. At present no operators have decided to extend this refurbishment to other Class 144 units, preferring instead to commit to new replacement DMU trains.

Class 150 No. 150109 Vehicle No. 52109

While the Pacer units were constructed using bus parts and intended for short journeys, British Rail intended the Sprinter units to be used for medium to long-distance services. They were based on the successful Mk 3 coach, which was built by BREL Derby between 1975 and 1985. The first Class 150 units built were two prototypes in 1984. The first unit, No. 150001, featured a Cummins NT855R5 engine with Voith transmission. The second prototype, No. 150002, featured a Rolls-Royce engine with Self Changing Gears transmission. No. 150001 was the clear winner and proved itself to be the more reliable of the two prototypes. Metro-Cammell also produced two prototype Sprinter units. They were designated Class 151 units but were not reliable enough and no orders followed. After the prototypes were evaluated, an order for fifty Class 150 units was placed with BREL. No. 150109 is pictured at Doncaster station wearing Provincial two-tone blue livery with white stripe. She would later receive West Midlands PTE Centro livery and currently operates in London Midland livery.

Class 150 No. 150133 Vehicle No. 52133

All of the prototype Sprinter units were built as three-car units. The production Class 150 units were built with only two coaches. The first fifty Class 150 units, designated Class 150/1 units, did not feature end gangway doors. By 1989 it was decided to strengthen some of the Class 150/1 units by inserting a Class 150/2 vehicle between the two Class 150/1 vehicles. The Class 150/2 vehicles had been constructed with end gangway connections. No. 150133 is one such unit that was reformed into a three-car unit using vehicle No. 52218. Pictured at Blackpool North station, the unit wears Regional Railways Greater Manchester PTE livery, which suited these units well. The unit would later be reformed back into a two-car unit.

Class 150 No. 150143 Vehicle No. 52143

Another of the temporary three-car Class 150 units, No. 150143 is pictured at Platform 5 in Lancaster station. The guard can be seen talking to the driver in the driving cab as he sets the train up ready to depart to Manchester Victoria. The additional coach inserted between the Class 150/1 vehicles is Class 150/2 vehicle No. 57253. Another benefit of fitting an additional Class 150/2 vehicle was the extra guard's door control panel, which would enable the guard to operate doors from the centre coach of the train as well as the end cabs. No. 150143 is pictured in Provincial Sprinter livery and would later receive Northern Rail livery. A feature of the Class 150/1 units was a manual, inward-opening crew door at each end. The later Class 150/2 units featured an air-operated sliding door.

Class 150 No. 150215 Vehicle No. 57215

The next batch of Class 150 units ordered were designated Class 150/2 units and eighty-five two-car units were constructed by BREL York between 1986 and 1987. Visually, the main differences with the Class 150/2 units compared to the Class 150/1 units was the provision of a front-end gangway and air-operated sliding crew doors. Many of the Class 150/2 units would be split to strengthen Class 150/1 units into three-coach trains. No. 150215 is pictured at Blackpool North station and is wearing Provincial Network Northwest livery. The unit entered service in Provincial Sprinter livery before receiving Provincial Network Northwest livery in 1991. By 1993 she had been repainted into Greater Manchester PTE livery and would go on to receive First Northwestern livery and Northern Rail livery.

Class 150 No. 150216 Vehicle No. 57216

Pictured at Cardiff Central station, Class 150 No. 150216 is wearing West Midland PTE Centro livery. She would later receive First Great Western livery and is now based in the West Country. Station staff can be seen wearing the traditional BR Hi-Viz clothing of the time while picking up litter from the track. An InterCity-liveried Mk 3 HST set can be seen in the background.

Class 150 No. 150252 Vehicle No. 52252

No. 150252 is pictured wearing Provincial Sprinter livery at North Berwick station while getting ready to head back to Edinburgh Haymarket, the location of her home depot. She would go on to receive Scotrail National Express livery before being transferred to Wales in May 2005. Scotrail lost all twelve of their Class 150 units to Wales in May 2005. No. 150252 is now part of the Arriva Trains Wales fleet and wears Arriva corporate livery. North Berwick is located at the end of a branch line and was electrified as part of the ECML electrification program.

Class 950 No. 9550001 Vehicle No. 999600

One final Class 150 unit was constructed in 1987. This two-car unit was built for the BR Civil Engineers to use as a track assessment unit. She was originally numbered as a Class 180 unit but with the introduction of the Great Western Class 180 Adelante in 2000, she was re-designated a Class 950 unit. She can still be found operating around the network today and now wears Network Rail all-over yellow livery. No. 950001 is pictured at York Station. The yellow boxes that can be seen to the side of the unit are battery-charging units.

Class 153 No. 153311 Vehicle No. 52311

The Class 153 units began life as Class 155 units. They were constructed between 1987 and 1988 by British Leyland at their Workington plant and, like some of the earlier-built Pacer units, they featured Leyland National bus parts. In 1990, BR decided to convert all thirty-five Class 155 units into seventy Class 153 single-car units. The contract was awarded to Hunslet Barclay, Kilmarnock, and the conversion work was carried out between 1991 and 1992. No. 153311 is pictured inside the main workshop at Kilmarnock and is nearing completion. During the conversion work, the units were outshopped in Regional Railways livery. She later received East Midlands Trains livery and is still an active member of their fleet today. For a while she carried the name *John Constable*.

Class 153 No. 153328 Vehicle No. 52328

The major part of the conversion work involved constructing a new driving cab at one end of each coach. To avoid moving the position of the entrance doors on the units, it was decided to fit the new cab into the remaining available space. This resulted in a very cramped cab, which is noticeably smaller than the original cab. Many train crews were unhappy about the size of the cab and some depots refused to work the Class 153 units. No. 153328 is pictured outside the main Hunslet Barclay workshop at Kilmarnock, ready to return back into service. She is fresh from the paint shop and looks smart in Regional Railways livery. This photograph shows the newly constructed cab, a noticeable feature of which was the vertical hinge fitted to the middle of the flyscreen door. No. 153328 would go on to receive Arriva Trains livery, followed by Northern Rail livery. Today she remains part of the Northern rail fleet.

Class 153 No. 153367 Vehicle No. 57367

The thirty-five Class 155 units were formed of vehicles numbered 52301–52335 and 57301–57335. After conversion to Class 153 units, vehicles numbered 52301–52335 became 153301–153335. Vehicles numbered 57301–57335 had fifty added to the vehicle numbers and became unit numbers 153351–153385, formed of vehicle numbers 57351–57385. No. 153367 is pictured inside the main workshop at Hunslet Barclay, Kilmarnock, and is having a few finishing touches added before she returns to service. She is pictured wearing Regional Railways livery and would later receive First Northwestern livery before receiving Arriva corporate livery after being transferred to Arriva Trains Wales.

Class 153 Vehicle Unknown

An unidentified Class 155 vehicle is pictured within the main workshop at Hunslet Barclay, Kilmarnock, undergoing conversion into a Class 153 unit. The unit is still wearing her Provincial Sprinter livery but would leave the works in Regional Railways livery. This photograph shows the volume of work involved in the conversion to a Class 153 unit, and when taken it can be seen that a new fiberglass front panel has been fitted, along with a gangway door. The first saloon window has also been removed and plated over but a lot of wiring work still has to be completed.

Class 155 No. 153324 Vehicle No. 57324

Class 155 No. 155324 is pictured in Provincial Sprinter livery shortly before undergoing conversion into a Class 153 unit. She is pictured inside the main workshop at Hunslet Barclay, Kilmarnock, and would later emerge as No. 153374, formed of vehicle No. 57374. While allocated to the West Country, she would carry a special all-over advert livery advertising great scenic railways of Devon and Cornwall. She was one of four units that were stored at Eastleigh in December 2006 but would later return to service with East Midland Trains, whose livery she now carries.

Class 155 No. 155341 Vehicle No. 52341

A further seven Class 155 units were ordered in 1988. These units were owned by West Yorkshire PTE and did not undergo conversion into Class 153 units. All seven units are based at Neville Hill depot in Leeds and can be found operating services between Leeds, Harrogate and York. No. 155341 is pictured at Leeds station while wearing West Yorkshire PTE red and cream livery, but she would later receive Northern Rail livery complete with Metro branding. The windows fitted to Class 155 units were smaller than those fitted to other Sprinter units, which meant that the units featured more windows on each coach and in turn looked longer that other units. They were in fact 23 meters long – the same length as a Class 156 vehicle.

Class 155 No. 155345 Vehicle No. 57345

When the Class 155 units were first introduced into service in 1987, they experienced a lot of issues with their passenger entrance doors. The units featured a style of sliding plug door, which was a first for British Rail DMUs. Intended to give a smooth, stylish look to the bodyside when compared to other DMUs being constructed at the time, there were incidents of them opening while the train was in motion. This resulted in the entire Class 155 fleet being grounded until modifications could be carried out to the door mechanism. Class 156 units temporarily took over the Class 155 duties until the Class 155 units returned to service in November 1989. After the modifications to the doors, the units settled down to become reliable units. Unit No. 155345, another unit owned by West Yorkshire PTE, is pictured in West Yorkshire PTE livery while departing from Preston station.

Class 156 No. 156481 Vehicle No. 52481

The Class 155 and Class 156 units were known as 'Super Sprinters'. They were intended for longer-distance services and had a top speed of 75 mph. While the Class 155 units were constructed by British Leyland, the Class 156 units were built by Metro-Cammell at Washwood Heath, near Birmingham, between 1987 and 1989. Metro-Cammell had already produced a prototype DMU, known as a Class 151, of which two were built. For the Class 156 units, Metro-Cammell reverted to a more conservative design. The front ends featured a gangway door and they were similar in appearance to Class 150 and Class 155 units. The Class 156 units were also constructed out of steel and had a single leaf entrance door at the body ends rather than pairs of doors mid-way. It was felt this was better suited to the type of work these units would be employed on. The first unit entered service at Norwich on 10 November 1987. Between December 1988 and November 1989, twenty-five Class 156 units were sent to Cardiff to temporarily replace the Class 155 units that were required to undergo modifications to their door systems. No. 156481 is pictured passing through Doncaster station, heading for Sheffield. She is wearing the Provincial Sprinter livery she received when she first entered service. She is currently part of the Northern Rail fleet and has carried two different Northern liveries so far.

Class 156 No. 156501 Vehicle No. 52501

In total, 114 Class 156 units were constructed. The first 100 were delivered in Provincial Sprinter livery, while the last fourteen received Strathclyde PTE orange and black livery. No. 156501 was the first unit to be delivered in SPT livery. This livery suited these units well and they carried this livery until around 1997, at which point they received a red and carmine version of SPT livery. All have now been repainted into standard Scotrail livery. No. 156502 travelled to the Netherlands in June 1989 to take part in celebrations to mark 150 years of the Dutch railways. Upon her return to the UK she was fitted with yellow NL stickers on her second-man-side destination boxes. No. 156501 is pictured in Platform 1 at Kilmarnock station awaiting departure to Glasgow Central. Little did I realise when I took this photograph, that many years later I would regularly drive this same unit over the same route between Kilmarnock and Glasgow Central.

Class 156 No. 156504 Vehicle No. 57504

The fourteen Class 156 Strathclyde PTE-liveried units were intended for use on Strathclyde PTE services around the Glasgow area; however, in reality they could be found anywhere on the Scotrail network, including Carlisle or even Newcastle. Class 156 No. 156504 is pictured at BRML Springburn works and appears to have been involved in a minor collision around the driver-side entrance door. The destination display is showing Kyle of Lochalsh, but it is not known if the unit ever operated on the Inverness to Kyle of Lochalsh line. If it had operated on the Kyle of Lochalsh line or anywhere north of Inverness, it would require fitting with RETB (Radio Electronic Token Block) radios. The red and white striped flag that can be seen inside the driver's windscreen is an indication that an important item of safety equipment has been isolated on the unit.

Class 158 No. 158705 Vehicle No. 52705

The final class of second generation DMUs produced in the 1980s were the Class 158 units. They were constructed between 1989 and 1992 at BREL, Derby. In total, 182 Class 158 units were built, including ten units for West Yorkshire PTE. A further twenty-two Class 158 units were converted to Class 159 units at Rosyth dockyard prior to entering service. After the Provincial sector placed the order for the Class 158s, a downturn in the economy meant they no longer required all the units ordered. At this time Network SouthEast required new DMUs and so agreed to take the surplus Class 158 units. In 2006 a further eight Class 158s were converted to Class 159 units. The Class 158 units were approximately a year late into service due to technical problems. The units were constructed from aluminium and were therefore lightweight. They featured disc brakes and it was quickly found that during the annual leaf-fall season, a build-up of leaf mulch on the wheels caused the Class 158 units to fail to operate signalling track circuits. During autumn 1992, many Class 158 units were split and reformed with Class 156 vehicles that featured conventional tread brakes, thus alleviating the problem. Over time the Class 158 units were fitted with scrubber blocks to keep the wheels free of leaf mulch. The first Class 158 units were allocated to Scotland and took over Express services between Glasgow, Edinburgh, Inverness and Aberdeen. A nearly new Class 158 unit, No. 158705, is pictured in Platform 5 at Perth station. She is wearing Provincial Express livery, which suited these units well.

Class 158 No. 158721 Vehicle No. 57721

The first thirty-three Class 158 units were built with a fifteen-seat first class section within the coach. They were all allocated to Scotland from new and continue to be allocated to Scotrail. During 2016 and 2017 the first class sections were removed from all Scotrail Class 158 units. In this photograph of No. 158721 taken at Inverkeithing when fairly new, a yellow stripe denoting first class can be seen above the rear coach windows. The Class 158 units were fitted with three different engines. Nos 158701–158814 were fitted with 350 hp Cummins engines. Nos 158815–158862 were fitted with 350 hp Perkins engines, with Nos 158863–158872 receiving 400 hp Cummins engines. The reason for the final ten Class 158 units receiving more powerful engines was to enable the units to cope with the gradients on the Welsh Marches line.

Class 158 No. 158803 Vehicle unknown

Like the other Sprinter-type trains, the Class 158 units were formed into two-car formation sets. Seventeen Class 158s, however, received a third coach. The centre vehicles were numbered 58701–58717. They were added to units 158798–158814 and initially allocated to Heaton depot, near Newcastle, for use on the Trans-Pennine services. Three-car-formed No. 158803 is pictured in Provincial Express livery at Manchester Victoria station. In 2006 she was one of eight three-car Class 158 units modified at Wabtec Doncaster to become Class 159 units. She received fleetnumber 159102 and was transferred to operate with Southwest Trains, based at Salisbury depot.

Class 165 No. 165002 Vehicle No. 58802

The Class 165 units, known as Network Turbo units, were constructed by BREL York between 1990 and 1992. In total seventy-six units were built. The first thirty-nine units were designated Class 165/0 units and had a top speed of 75 mph, and eleven were constructed as three-car units. The final thirty-seven units were designated Class 165/1 units and had a top speed of 90 mph; seventeen of which were three-car units. They were designed to operate on services from London Marylebone and London Paddington stations, replacing the first generation DMUs, and were branded either Thames Turbos (Paddington services) or Chiltern Turbos (Marylebone services). To take advantage of the wider gauge on the lines they operate over, they were constructed as wide-bodied units and are 2.81 metres wide compared to 2.7 metres wide for a Class 158 unit. A purpose-built depot was opened at Aylesbury on 14 May 1991 and No. 165002 is pictured within the depot shortly after to facilitate staff training. Due to a downturn in the economy she was one of seven Class 165 units transferred in 1993 from Aylesbury to Thames Trains' Reading depot. In 2004 she was transferred back to Chiltern Trains, where she remains an active member of the fleet.